yoga
reminder

yoga reminder

Lightened Reflections

A. G. Mohan

with Dr. Ganesh Mohan

Edited by Nitya Mohan and Patty Moynahan

ISBN: 978-981-09-4338-7 (paperback)

Svastha Yoga
www.svastha.net

Gratitude.

To the yoga sages of the millennia past, for their timeless wisdom that is a beacon for clarity and well-being in our lives.

To the yoga teachers and practitioners in the present, for their dedication and enthusiasm in keeping that message alive and growing.

Contents

Introduction

Millions of people around the world now engage in various practices that go by the name of yoga. From sleepy hamlets to bustling cities, practitioners are experiencing the benefits of yoga. Many people—including millions of yoga students—think of yoga as simply a series of stretching exercises. It has even become a competitive sport! A great many consider yoga a method of relaxation. Some think that yoga is an alternative treatment for physical diseases and mental disorders. Still others view it as a way to tap into esoteric knowledge. And certain critics of yoga view it as a set of cultic religious practices.

In its original statement and intent, yoga is not an abstract concept, such as happiness, that often means different things to different individuals. Its basic objectives are timeless and ageless. Yoga is the means to bring a positive shift in the basal well-being of the mind and the body.

What I present in this book may appear to be a new way of thinking about yoga, but it is actually a very *old* way of thinking about it.

Because yoga's original meaning and purpose has become obscured, the practice of yoga has become diluted and often perplexing. This shift is unfortunate—especially now—because the practice of yoga as it was developed many centuries ago offers a wonderfully comprehensive antidote to frenzied modern lives, which are often stress laden, self-focused, and over-stimulated.

If you currently take classes that are called yoga, the information in this book will help you determine whether you are actually doing a yoga practice aligned with its original intent and methods. You might well ask, "Does it really matter whether I'm doing yoga? I enjoy my classes."

The premise of this book is that it does matter. It is in your best interest to be clear about what you are doing and why you are doing it. The practice of yoga should not be a matter of blind faith in a teacher or in the teaching.

This book is not an attempt to convert you to yet another brand of yoga or to dissuade you from your present classes. Instead, this book aims to encourage active, ongoing inquiries into the practice of yoga by students and teachers alike.

My hope is that whatever practice you undertake is informed and enriched by alert curiosity, clear and well-reasoned thinking, common sense, and personal experience.

1 *Minding Your Mind*

Update Your Software: Minding Your Self

We are functioning organisms, every one of us, with a mind and a body. Like a computer has software running on hardware, we have many functions running on our bodies and brains.

Think of yoga as a way to maintain the hardware and update the software of the body and mind.

But you don't have to practice yoga to receive updates to your body-mind software. The experiences in our lives are continually updating our bodies and minds These automatic updates are out of our control. Sometimes they result in improvements; sometimes they degrade the system.

Fortunately, it is possible to intentionally and positively revise our mental and physical programs in a way that leads to health and happiness. This opportunity is the possibility—and the promise—of yoga.

Hardwired for Happiness?

Our unconscious mental and physical updates are largely based on this universal wish: "I want to live happily forever."

When we say this, by "I" we mean our bodies and minds. By "happily" we mean in such a way that we get what we want, experience pleasure, and avoid pain. By "forever" we mean an unchanging, everlasting continuum of pleasure.

The search for happiness begins in infancy and leads to a repeating cycle of pleasure and pain throughout our lives.

An infant feels the pangs of hunger. She becomes unhappy and cries. When she nurses at her mother's breast, her crying stops. She is happy again.

A child covets his playmate's new toy. The playmate will not share the toy, so the child becomes unhappy. When the child's parents buy him the toy, he is happy.

A teenager has a crush on a boy, but the boy seems not to notice her, so she is unhappy. When the boy finally discovers the girl, she is happy.

An adult dislikes his job and is unhappy. When he gets his dream job, he becomes happy.

An older adult wishes to live closer to her family. When her son invites her to live with his family, she becomes happy.

But things can and do change in our lives.

The child's new toy breaks. The teenager's boyfriend leaves her for another girl. The adult loses his dream job. The older adult can no longer climb the stairs to her bedroom in her son's house. All of these developments are external changes that interrupt happiness.

Coupled with these external influences are the internal changes that interrupt happiness. The mind changes, too. The child loses interest in the toy and wants another one. The teenager becomes bored with her boyfriend and is attracted to someone else. The adult loses interest in his career and wants a more exciting one. The older adult convinces herself that her family is ignoring her needs.

An American student of mine told me that when he was a young man, his father gave him this prescription for a happy life: "By the age of thirty, you should have two houses—one in the city and one in the country—two kids, two cars, and a million dollars in the bank." My student said, "At thirty, I had achieved all of those things. But I was not happy!"

A SHORT STORY

"Will you marry me?" he asked.

"No," she replied.

And they lived happily after.

~~~~~~~~~

Absence of change can also lead to unhappiness. How happy would a parent be if his two-year-old child remained two years old for several years?

Everything in the material world changes. And this fundamental fact—that everything in the external world is always changing in one way or another—suggests that there will always be a cycle of happiness and unhappiness for us. Likewise, because our minds are always changing, we are likely to experience cycles of happiness and unhappiness throughout our lives.

But this inevitability does not have to be so.

External circumstances are partially, and often totally, out of our control. But internal changes are within our control.

To control internal changes, though, it is important to know what we are dealing with when we speak of the mind.

~~~~~~~~~

LEAVE EVERYTHING BEHIND

A man once visited a sage, claiming that he wanted to become a monk—that is, he wanted to renounce his life as a householder and retreat to the forest to pursue his spiritual quest. The man explained to the guru that his life had too many distractions and problems. He wanted to leave all the annoyances of his home life and begin a spiritual journey.

The sage said, "You want to pursue your spiritual path, and that is a noble goal. You want to leave everything in your life behind and start a new journey. But tell me, where are you going to leave your mind?"

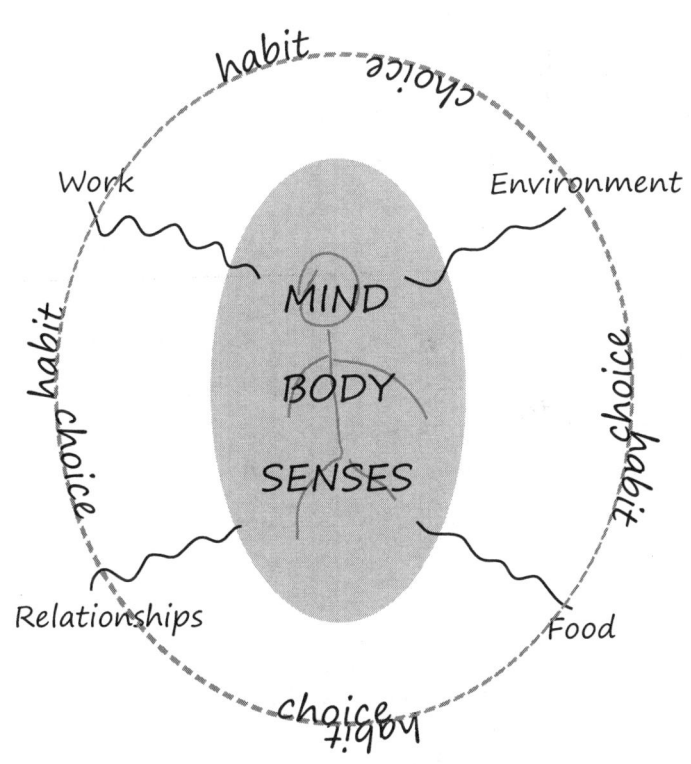

Our mind-body-senses are constantly
updated, unconsciously by habit and
consciously by our choices!

What Is "Mind"?

What we call *mind* is the patterns of thoughts and feelings that repeat throughout our lives. These patterns are largely unconscious and operate automatically.

These patterns are constantly modified, strengthened, or weakened by our bodily and sense actions and by our thoughts and feelings themselves.

The patterns can produce pleasure, as, for example, when a child who is cared for by a loving parent comes to associate a feeling of pleasure with the appearance of the parent. Or when a man who has derived deep satisfaction from gazing at paintings feels an immediate sense of pleasure as he walks into an art museum.

However, many of our patterns can produce unhappiness and pain. For example, a girl who has a painful tooth extraction might thereafter associate a feeling of dread with going to the dentist. Or a person who has formed the expectation that she should be unconditionally accepted might feel wounded by any perceived rejection.

Three Parts of the Mind

The mind consists of three components arranged in a hierarchy:

- the storage system,

- the intellect, and

- the I-sense.

The most basic level of mind is the storage system, where our sensory impressions and experiences are collected and retained as complexes of thoughts, feelings, and actions. When these complexes come into our awareness, we call them memories. Next is the intellect, which processes information and makes images (composed of thoughts, feelings, and actions) of the world around us and the world within us. The intellect allows us to make nuanced judgments about what is "good" or "desirable" and what is "bad" or "undesirable."

The highest component of the mind is the I-sense. The I-sense governs our decisions to act or to refrain from acting: "I will do this," or "I will not do this."

Here is an example of how the three components work together. Suppose that on a neighborhood walk, we see something ahead on the sidewalk. Our storage system recognizes this something as a puppy. The storage system also recognizes (from past experiences and the memories stored as a result of them) that the puppy seems lost and frightened and recalls our protective feelings toward vulnerable creatures.

The storage system sends a message to our intellect, which assembles the different aspects of the scene and makes a judgment about it that we would like to pick up the puppy and comfort it. The intellect is ready to send a message to our body to do that. Then the I-sense makes the executive decision whether to act on this judgment—whether to actually pick up the puppy.

Ordinarily, though, we are not conscious of the interaction among these three components.

For example, when we reach the driveway of our house, we usually are not aware that our storage system is accessing the imprinted memory of the house, our intellect is confirming that the house is "good" because it is ours, and the I-sense is driving the decision to enter the house.

Sometimes it can seem that only one or two components are operating. For example, when we see a snake, most of us immediately react with fear. There's no awareness of the I-sense weighing the options, as in, "Should I approach the snake or run?" We run. In fact, research suggests that the fear of snakes may be hardwired in humans and other mammals, which accounts for our reflexive response to snakes as threats.

And, as a final example, we may act impulsively, without consciously considering the wisdom of our actions until we've taken them, as in, "Why did I eat that third piece of chocolate cake?"

Each of the three components of the mind contains representations of patterns of thoughts, feelings, and actions that we have repeated throughout our lives.

Not the usual response!

The unconscious operations of our minds can at times work against us. They can cause us to repeat patterns of thought, feeling, and action that result in our unhappiness and pain. They can be sources of addictions as well as impediments to healthy relationships. They can sabotage our best intentions and plans.

Fortunately for us, we don't have to be victims of the unconscious operations of these components. We can become aware of these operations of our minds and exert some control over them. It takes time and practice because it involves the exercise of vigilance and discipline over our perceptions, judgments, and choices.

After all, we have the capacity to exercise control, and we do so depending on the situation. If we are invited to our friend's house for dinner, we will choose to speak in our own way. If we are invited to have dinner at the White House, we will exercise vigilance and speak in a different way.

Minding the mind in this way enhances steadiness and strength, and brings in calmness and clarity, and those lead to the long-term rewards of happiness and peace.

MY SOUL MATE

"I am on the lookout for my soul mate," an American told me.

I told him, "If you understand what your soul is, you will realize that it doesn't need a mate. When your mind changes, your mate may change. Do not look for a soul mate; make your mind steady."

Mental Steadiness

Mental steadiness is the ability to hold in the mind a peaceful thought of one's choice and allow it to come into the mind again and again. In time one is able to hold on to the peaceful thought even while facing adversity.

Unless we cultivate the ability to choose one peaceful thought over other thoughts, we will not be happy, even if all of our wishes are fulfilled.

This failure is due to the changing nature of our minds. We will constantly fear losing what we have gained.

Long ago, a man went into the forest alone and sat under a tree. He didn't know that he was sitting under a tree that fulfilled wishes. The man casually wished for a thousand gold coins. Suddenly, the coins appeared. The man's surprise and happiness were quickly replaced by fear and worry. He was alone in the forest with a treasure and was therefore easy prey for thieves who would want to steal the treasure. And, sure enough, thieves did come and steal the man's coins.

Mental steadiness is not optional. We all need it.

Three Modes of Operation

We have three general modes of operation in our minds. The first mode is characterized by feelings of lightness and brightness, contentment, quiet, and clarity. It is not exultation but the feeling of contentment and completeness that stems from a tranquil mind.

The less we experience fluctuations in the mind, the greater the depth of completeness and contentment we feel.

It is a state of mind that arises because of a decrease in the mental fluctuations caused by desire—either temporarily by the fulfillment of a particular desire or more permanently through the means suggested by yoga. Wellness and peace go along with it.

Such feelings are indicators of our health and are always accompanied by kindness, compassion, and contentment. All of us aspire for this state—complete and fulfilled. In this mode, our minds are like still, clear water.

The next mode is characterized by excitement or stimulation—by excess mental activity, obsession, agitation, and lack of control. In this mode, we are likely to be angry, contentious, and controlling. It is a state of mind in which desire or dislike drives us to action.

Contact with some object, person, or situation, or simply the memory of it in our minds, evokes feelings of desire or dislike. On this basis, we act either to attain or to avoid that object, person, or situation.

We do not have a choice in this matter because we will be unhappy if we do not act. If we have the necessary skills and knowledge, and if the circumstances are favorable, we will successfully attain what we desire or avoid or remove what we dislike. Our minds are like rushing water.

~~~~~~~~~~

JUST A MINUTE

A resident of New York called the airline office and asked, "What is the flying time to Los Angeles?"

The airline rep said, "Just a minute."

The New Yorker said, "Thank you," and hung up.

~~~~~~~~~~

The third mode is one of heaviness or dullness, insatiability and delusion, and lack of control. In this mode, we are likely to take action without thinking or to take no action at all. We may

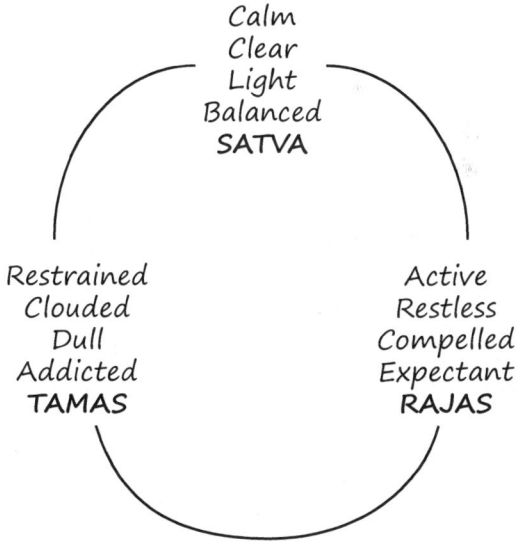

Calm
Clear
Light
Balanced
SATVA

Restrained
Clouded
Dull
Addicted
TAMAS

Active
Restless
Compelled
Expectant
RAJAS

The mind, body, and senses
cycle through these three modes.

face a situation in which we are not clear about what to do to satisfy our desire or reduce our unhappiness.

When our minds are not clear, we may not act when we should, or we may act when we should not. This mode manifests as inactivity or retarded activity. Our mind is like still, muddy water.

~~~~~~~~~

CAR THIEVES!

The phone rings at a police station, and a policeman picks it up to hear someone say, "Thieves have been at work in my car. They've stolen the steering wheel, gearbox, and clutch." The policeman notes the address and is about to leave when the phone rings again. "It's me again. Sorry, sir; I got into the rear by mistake."

~~~~~~~~~

The Flux of Mental Modes

There is always an interaction among the three modes of the mind. The interaction among modes produces the basic emotions of desire and aversion, from which all other emotions derive.

For example, when a thought arises in our minds, we can say that the active mode is at work. When that thought disappears, we say that the dull mode has pulled it down. When we retain a thought of our choice clearly and for a long time, we say that the stillness and clarity mode is dominating.

This cycle goes on constantly and unconsciously in our minds. Consequently, we are always alternating between contentment and desire, clarity and confusion.

Our state of mind is naturally altered by time and by the object we are thinking about. We may associate one state of mind with a certain object or person at a particular time, but our relationship to the same object or person may change over time so that the object or person later induces a different state of mind.

Therefore these modes are not absolutes that pervade our minds. Rather, our minds constantly shift among the three modes in varying intensities. All three modes are always present in our minds, but at any moment, one will be stronger than the others, only to be overshadowed by the ascension of another.

From this constant fluctuation and rotation in our minds, it naturally follows that the modes are not fixed character traits, though some of us may have a predominance of one over the others. That is, we all have all these states of mind to varying degrees.

CANNOT LIVE WITHOUT YOU

John to Mary at twenty years: "I cannot live without you."

John to Mary at thirty years: "I cannot live with you."

The Desirable Mode

We could describe the three modes of the mind in short as calm, restless, and clouded. The first (calm) mode is the most desirable, and the second and third modes represent aberrations or deviations from this state. To understand why, let us look a little further into how the state of mind from which we act affects the outcomes of our actions and therefore their successes or failures. When the first mode is dominant in our minds, we act with awareness and calmness, undisturbed by the possible failure or success of the action. Our mental balance is not dependent on the outcome of the action because we do not bind our happiness and contentment to our success. This approach allows us to act or not to act with equal ease.

That is, we not only have the ability to act with calm efficiency but are also free from the compulsion to act. We can withdraw with no misgivings if that is what needs to be done.

When we act from the first mode, we can do what is required—no more and no less—and never lose our mental calm.

When the restless mode dominates our minds, we will act with vigor and compulsion, and expectation and anxiety regarding the outcome of the action will color our minds. Our happiness is bound to the outcome. We feel that we will be happier if the outcome is successful. That is, the underlying feeling of discontent drives the action. The anxiety, expectation, and drive to act affect our mental calm and hamper our ability to act with balance.

JUMPING TO CONCLUSIONS

The eagle-eyed owner of a company walked through his shipping department one day and noticed a boy lounging against a box and reading a comic book.

"How much do you get a week?" he asked the boy grimly.

"Fifty dollars, sir." The owner handed him a fifty-dollar bill and said, "Here is a week's pay. Now get out." As the boy left, the angry man turned to the head of the shipping department and snapped, "When did you hire him?"

"Never, sir" was the reply. "He just brought some packages from another firm and was waiting for his receipt."

When the clouded mode dominates our minds, we lack clarity about what we should or should not do. This confusion results in inaction or inappropriate action.

When the restless and clouded modes are excessive, we can experience compulsive thinking and behavior, such as that exhibited by an alcoholic, drug addict, or food addict. The craving can be temporarily satisfied by alcohol, sedating drugs, or food, only to arise again unless the cycle is broken through mental steadiness.

Yoga Is the Means to the Desirable Mode

Yoga suggests that sustained effort can bring about lasting changes in our state of mind that will lead to greater contentment (the desirable mode).

We can always relate to an object in such a way that the balance of our minds is not disturbed.

Balance and clarity are a state of mind; they do not arise from the objects we come in contact with. They arise because of our minds' response to such contact.

To be in the desirable state is to instill in our minds such deep and unshakable steadiness that our balance, contentment, and clarity are not compromised by our interactions with objects, people and situations. To do this, the second and third modes need to be decreased, as they indicate a descent into imbalance and a lack of clarity.

Yoga deals in great detail with the means to achieve this balance so that we can move from our present state of fluctuating contentment to a state of greater quietness and tranquility.

All of us wish to always feel a sense of wellness. This desire is related to the first mode, characterized by lightness of body and brightness and clarity in our minds. To further our mental health and balance, to know what will bring us and others happiness, and to act on this knowledge with maximum clarity, we need to develop the first mode in preference to the second and third modes.

This is yoga.

Three Modes in the Body and Senses, Too

These three modes of operation also pervade our bodies and senses as well.

Wellness of body and mind is characterized by awakening in the morning with a feeling of lightness and clarity. (Otherwise, we may need several cups of coffee to get going!) During the day, we need to maintain the feeling of lightness and clarity in all of our activities in order to function at our best.

For example, when we are tired and have sore muscles, we can go to a massage therapist. If done properly, the massage will bring back a feeling of lightness and brightness in our body and dispel our fatigue. However, if the therapist extends the massage to several hours, we will experience pain again. This is why a mindless yoga practice or a mindful but incorrectly performed practice can result in harm.

We could listen to our favorite piece of music for an hour, but how pleasant would it be to listen to it for ten hours? This is because our senses are also characterized by the three modes of operation.

Our mental modes are also affected by diet. Proper nutrition is essential to maintain a clear mind!

~~~~~~~~~~

MY APPENDIX

While the diagnosis of the patient who had eaten and drunk rather generously was proceeding, the sick man asked, "Doctor, do you think the trouble is in my appendix?"

"Oh no," said the doctor, "the trouble is in your table of contents."

~~~~~~~~~~

Updating our mental software involves updating our bodily and sensory software.

The Monkey Mind

If we give our minds free rein, they become what the ancient sages likened to a drunken monkey that has been stung by a scorpion. This comparison is deeper than it initially seems.

First, it is the nature of a monkey to jump around. Even if the monkey is trained, it will retain its innate nature and will not become as focused as, say, a trained horse.

Second, drinking alcohol is a self-inflicted illness. We often assault our own minds.

Third, being stung by a scorpion is an affliction from an external source.

Apples! Grapes! Bananas!
Decision time for the monkey mind.

So it is with our minds and bodies. Our minds are inconstant, and we are assaulted by ills from within and without.

Attachment and Aversion

The thoughts and feelings that arise in the mind are usually the product of two fundamental emotions: attraction and aversion (desire and dislike). All other emotions are related to these two. We seek what gives us pleasure (attraction) and avoid what causes us harm (aversion).

The I-sense generates the thoughts associated with attachment and aversion: I want...I like...I don't want...I don't like... This I-sense is usually associated with the body, mind, and the senses and is also continually under the influence of external events. Social networking websites are examples of this sense in action!

According to yoga, thinking and emotions are the root of behavior; action follows.

Without awareness and self-control, our thoughts and feelings become actions without any filters, and we become enslaved by them.

To become free, we must interrupt the cycle that generates impulsive and compulsive behavior.

~~~~~~~~~

INSIDER THEFT

There once was a man whose job was to walk the streets of his village each night, banging a drum and calling out, "Thieves, beware!" The villagers slept peacefully each night, knowing that their belongings were safe from thieves.

One day, however, the man became ill. The man's son offered to take his father's place that night. As the son walked the streets of the village, he banged the drum and called out a warning.

But instead of calling out, "Thieves, beware!" the son called out, "Beware of the thieves, desire, anger, and fear, inside each of you! They are stealing your freedom!"

~~~~~~~~~

All of us are subject to the diseases of compulsive and obsessive thinking, in which we feel at the mercy of our thoughts. This condition can happen when, for example, we become infatuated with someone, when we feel resentful toward someone whom we believe has injured us. At these times, our minds are like a dog with a bone.

When we find ourselves caught in this type of thinking, we try to use force to banish the thinking. As we know, this approach only makes the situation worse.

Aversion is a deep attachment.

Cognitive research has shown that conscious suppression of a thought is not effective. A popular illustration is the command, "Don't think about a pink elephant!"

Yoga is a means to attain freedom from repetitive cycles of harmful thinking that cause suffering. This process requires us to use our free will to slow down and recognize arising thoughts—particularly thoughts that lead to compulsive and harmful actions such as overeating, substance abuse, and violence. If we allow the cycle of harmful thoughts to continue, our future will be a repetition of our past. We will then be living under a form of tyranny of our own making.

We do not try to stop the mind altogether because stopping the mind is not possible for most people. Instead, we strengthen our minds by developing the first mode: calm and light. We thus enhance our mental health and are less and less affected by external circumstances in our life.

Just as we cannot stop the activity of the mind altogether, we cannot necessarily reduce our desires. But through yoga, we can reduce the intensity of our desires, much like a carpenter who planes a piece of wood to make it smooth.

Intelligent focus and effort, not esoteric techniques, are the foundation of yoga.

We develop an awareness of what is going on in our minds so that we can let go of thoughts or place a distance between our thoughts and our actions. Even doing so in a small way is beneficial.

~~~~~~~~~~

IT TAKES TIME

A recently arrived Italian family was greatly and favorably impressed with America, especially the eight-year-old daughter. One day she announced that their neighbor had a new baby.

The mother told the daughter that she was mistaken; it must be an adopted baby because she had seen the neighbor only yesterday. The mother also explained the facts of life and that it took a baby nine months to arrive.

"Oh, but Mother," the girl said, "this is America."

~~~~~~~~~~

How Can We Update Our Mental Software?

You update your mental software by minding your mind: by bringing into your body, senses, and mind—and, indeed, your entire life—a feeling of lightness and clarity.

All of us have already experienced this feeling, if only briefly. In this state, our minds are clear and our comprehension is sharp. Our bodies feel healthy and free of tension or fatigue, and there is a sense of effortlessness in whatever we do.

This feeling is the gold standard by which we measure our progress toward minding our mind. The assessment of this progress is internal. However it will reflect in our external behavior.

The method for minding our minds was developed centuries ago. It is neither arcane nor mystical. Instead, it is logical, rational, and practical.

It is simple and straightforward but not easy. It requires conscious personal effort. But for those who choose this path, the effort is rewarded with health, longevity, and peace of mind. It is better to remind ourselves that there is really no choice.

Minding Your Mind:
Yogic Mindfulness

Awareness and attention must be present in every action; otherwise, the action becomes mechanical. When we speak of awareness and attention, there is the temptation to label yoga as a practice of mindfulness. But there is much confusion over this term.

Mindfulness—in the sense of paying close attention—is not in and of itself a virtue. For instance, one can mindfully drink a bottle of whiskey in one evening or eat an entire chocolate cake in one sitting. We can mindfully engage in a harmful practice of asanas when we attempt to do a headstand without proper preparation and instruction.

Without right knowledge, one can mindfully do a wrong practice.

True mindfulness is not just awareness of our actions. The phrase "minding the mind" rather than "mindfulness" better conveys the scope of watchfulness in yoga.

Minding the mind consists of observing the mind and bringing in the desirable mode that lead us to freedom from our own minds.

In fact, the ultimate aim of yoga is to go beyond the mind. So we can say that the highest achievement of yoga is mindlessness.

When faced with a problem, we can delude ourselves into thinking that we are "mindfully" considering the problem, when actually we are reinforcing the problem or obsessing over it. Minding your mind offers a way out of delusion. For example, when the mind is filled with thoughts of getting even with someone who has hurt me, is this a form of mindfulness? Or is it a form of bondage?

MINDFULLY GOING ASTRAY

A tailor suffering from insomnia finally agreed to try out the old remedy of counting sheep. The next morning he turned up for business more tired than ever. "What a night," he confessed. "I counted more than ten thousand sheep. Then I figured that they will yield thirty thousand yards of wool. That would make nine thousand suits, and where was I going to get all that lining?"

Mindfulness relates to a state of alert attention. Minding your mind is to bring balance, quietness, and peace. Minding your mind encompasses mindfulness.

Mindfulness is the first step in minding your mind.

In minding our minds, we need to watch how all our bodily actions and senses affect our minds and orient all our activities toward bringing about light. The purpose of the eight limbs of yoga is to bring about this light—the pathway to health, happiness, and peace.

Yoga is the path that leads us to our natural state of existence—the inner light.

~~~~~~~~~~

THE SOBER STATE

We are like the young bride of three months who complained to her relatives about her husband's drinking habits.

"If you knew he drank, why did you marry him?" they asked.

"I didn't know he drank," the girl replied, "until one night he came home sober."

~~~~~~~~~~

Thinking Is Behavior

There is no need to try to eliminate all thinking; it is not possible. But, for purposes of our mental stability, we need to remember that thinking is behavior.

Therefore, we should take the consequences of our thoughts as seriously as we take the consequences of our actions.

The update of this system is related to the practice of the do's of the don'ts (*yamas*) and the do's of the do's (*niyamas*). We need to fix an inner closed-circuit television and watch our minds.

Currently, we are like robots programmed to act based on our past actions.

We should not harbor negative thoughts. Negative thoughts are a weakness of our mind. The mental consequence of negative thoughts is to downgrade our mind. We should develop a regular practice of maintaining peaceful thoughts and insert such thoughts and feelings when we are irritable, angry, discouraged, or unmotivated.

This reprogramming takes conscious effort and practice, and it doesn't come out of the blue or in a state of ecstasy. And, most importantly, we have to do it ourselves.

No one else—not a guru or a loved one—can give us this ability. We have to help ourselves.

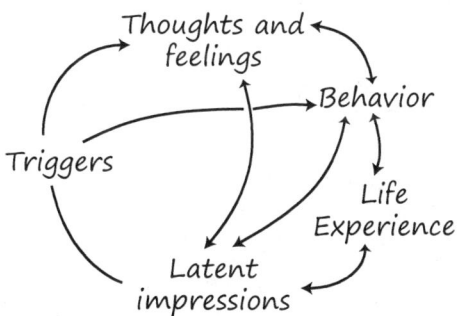

Life happens by way of this cycle.

QUIT IN BITS

An opium addict asked a wise man, "Can you help me quit? I have tried various methods. Everything has failed."

The wise man gave him a piece of chalk and told him, "Weigh your opium against this piece of chalk. The first time you weigh it, write 'one'; the next time, 'two'; and so on. Note how many times you have taken opium. See me after three months." The chalk started disappearing, though it was imperceptible in the beginning. Each time the quantity got reduced, but in a subtle way. Follow such an approach.

The Mind Is Not Alone

The mind is formless; it has no shape, color, touch, taste, sound, or smell. What we call the mind is an experience based on our thoughts and feelings.

We cannot make positive changes in the mind alone. We must modify the behavior pattern of all our subsystems.

The subsystems are our lower minds, our memories, the senses that give the input to our minds, our bodily actions, and the breath that links our bodies and minds.

Thus the eight limbs of yoga have practices involving and integrating each of these subsystems.

Minding the Senses

Our senses are the gateway to the outside world. Ideally, minding our senses is principally about minding our minds themselves. However, to start with, we need to restrain and retrain the behavior of our senses. For example, staring intently at an object of attraction makes our mind subservient to it.

We need to be careful what we feed our senses: what we eat, watch, and hear. Of course, the intent is not to repress or suppress but to manage intelligently so that the mind remains in the mode of calmness and clarity.

APPEASEMENT POLICY

Little John came home from school with a black eye.

"What have you been up to?" demanded his mother.

"I have been fighting with Paul," the boy confessed.

"Why?"

"I gave him only a small cake."

"Well, tomorrow take a bigger cake and make friends," his mother told him.

John did so, but the following afternoon returned with the other eye blackened.

"Good heavens! What happened?" shouted his mother.

"Paul wants more cake," replied John.

~~~~~~~~~~~

One important method in this context is the practice of pranayama. Pranayama allows us to draw our senses inward.

Sensory overload is a source of disturbance in our minds. Everything we see, hear, and touch leaves its mark on our mind. When our minds are overwhelmed by sensory information—for example, from television, smartphones, social media, the Internet, movies, or traffic—we become distracted (dis-tracted: "pulled apart").

If we reduce our exposure to such sensory noise in life, we are better able to think clearly and act more reasonably and responsibly.

When our minds are focused and under control, the senses obey the mind rather than the other way around. In some cases, external stimuli are unavoidable. In other cases, we can remove ourselves from them. A sound yoga practice teaches us to avoid filling our minds and senses with disturbing and harmful thoughts, images, and sounds.

Minding the Body and Breath

Our minds are housed in our bodies. We are our bodies. We are identified with our senses and bodies through our I-sense. We cannot wish this sense of identity away.

Through appropriate asana practice, it is possible to maintain good health and bring about lightness of body and brightness in the mind.

Our breath plays a key role, too, since it is linked to our mind, senses, and body. We begin this control of breath in asanas, and extend it in pranayama practice.

Can I Do It?

Yes, indeed. You can. Most importantly, only you can do it for yourself. If you do, you will have health and happiness.

No guru or loved one can do it for you. You have to help yourself.

It is in your hands.

DEAD OR ALIVE

A sage was confronted in his village by an arrogant young man who sought to prove that he was more clever than the sage. The young man had caught a bird and concealed it in his hand. He planned to ask the sage whether the bird was alive or dead. If the sage replied "dead," the young man would release the bird and allow it to fly away. If the sage replied "alive," the young man would wring the bird's neck to prove the sage wrong. The young man showed the sage the hand that concealed the bird. "Is the bird dead or alive?" he asked the sage.

The sage looked calmly into the eyes of the young man and replied, "It is in your hands."

2 *The Yoga Path*

Find Yourself

Yoga is an ancient philosophy, an ancient practice. The worldview of yoga is that our essential nature is of pure and calm awareness. That awareness is entangled in an ever-changing world through our mind, our senses, and our body. We are at peace within, in truth, though we may appear to be in pieces without! As the sage Vyasa says in his commentary on the Yogasutra:

The place in which the self is hidden is not to be found in the netherworlds, nor the mountain caves, nor darkness, nor the bottom of the oceans; it is in each thought.

Unfortunately, finding that peace within requires working through the chaos surrounding it—primarily through our own personal chaos generator: our minds. If we gradually bring our minds to a more focused state, we are better able to appreciate the calm within. Allow the mind to remain a mess, and that calm awareness within is nowhere to be seen.

But the pathway to our minds is from farther out: starting from our relationships, behavior, and actions and delving through our own body, deeper than the breath and even past the senses. Beyond all of these lies that intangible master of our inner world, the mind.

So yoga tells us that we must bring balance and clarity to all these layers of our life experience, and the mind will follow suit.

When we do manage to calm the mind, we experience that state of relaxed energy and awareness that is the defining essence of our real self. Yoga helps us find ourselves.

Focus and Then Unite

The root meaning of the word yoga can be derived in two ways, one being to unite (*yujir yoge*) and the other being to focus (*yuja samadhau*). The second meaning, to focus, is the one the Yogasutra chooses.

Yoga as union is a valuable ideal. The world could do with more unity today. Individuals could do with more unity within themselves. But as a practice guideline, unity is a vague concept.

Focus, while not so noble a goal in appearance, is a practical and effective guideline for practice. To bring steadiness and positivity to the mind; the body; the breath; and our senses, choices, and relationships—this is the goal of yoga. To bring this steadiness and positivity, we must ensure that we do not allow any of the above to be vagrant and scattered. In other words, finding steadiness requires focus.

I was fine until I got dizzy juggling them 12 times a minute in my mind.

Hence the Yogasutra defines the practice of yoga as focus of the mind. By cultivating that inner steadiness, we become beacons of positivity and balance, thus bringing about the more outward goal of unity in time.

From steadiness arises the possibility of holding to positivity. A scattered mind cannot stay focused on a positive goal.

From that positive and light mind, we bring cohesion to the body and breath. That cascades outward to our senses and choices and farther outward to our relationships, influencing those we are in contact with. Thus the greater goal of positive change and unity is also achieved.

Believe It or Not

Yoga may have evolved in ancient India, in the context of the traditions there, but the yoga of Patanjali is not synonymous with the religion of Hinduism and its many branches.

Religions come with a worldview, a philosophy, and a theosophy that a believer cannot reject.

Yoga has a practice and a philosophy. The practice is profoundly beneficial for body and mind. But the philosophy is optional.

By Patanjali's definition, yoga is a state of absolute calmness of the mind. The philosophy is an extension of this state, a statement of what one experiences as ultimate reality when the mind is in that calmness. But unlike in a religion, you are free to ignore this philosophy; that will diminish neither the somatic and psychological benefits of the practices nor the logic and framework behind the practices.

Religions expect compliance from their adherents. Religious precepts must be followed. But there is no compulsion for anyone to practice yoga. The yoga sages do not insist that one must do yoga. They present neither moral inducement nor fear of punishment. Instead, the Yogasutra merely points out that by doing these practices, we reduce the potential for unhappiness.

Practicing yoga is a wise choice, purely out of self-interest, but it is entirely the decision of each individual.

One religion cannot be practiced along with another, not with authenticity.

Yoga can be practiced along with any religion. It is just practices to focus and calm the mind, and steady and strengthen the body.

Religions are often faith systems that are averse to questioning. Authentic yoga welcomes questions. Practice when you understand clearly, says the Yogasutra, and your practice will be more effective.

I was giving a lecture in Washington, D.C. At the end of the lecture, a man in his sixties approached me and said, "Thanks to yoga, I can find quality cheaper wine." I did not understand.

He went on, "In the health food supermarket near my place, they keep the quality cheaper wine on the bottom rack. I found that out because after doing yoga for several years, I can now squat!"

〜〜〜〜〜

My Idol

The Yogasutra of Patanjali contains the practice of devotion to the Divine. The term devotion refers to an attitude of internal trust in and love for one's concept of the Divine.

Devotion, however, is an optional practice in the yoga path.

A practitioner is free to undertake a yoga practice on her own. Or she can seek the helping hand of the Divine, a being that is already in a state of permanent peace. It is as though she is floundering in the swift-flowing river of fluctuations in her own mind, and the Divine is on the riverbank, stable and peaceful. She can call to the Divine to help pull her out of the river.

Devotion as a practice can help support all the limbs of yoga, from asana through pranayama to control of the senses, and provide a deeply pleasant experience for meditation.

For the practice of devotion to work, though, our conception of the Divine has to be positive and nourishing.

Our idea of the Divine should have the best qualities that we want to see in our own minds. By connecting our minds to the qualities of such divinity, our thoughts and emotions will be guided toward a state of equanimity and freedom.

Some students gain inspiration from holding in their minds the thought of someone who has attained the state of spiritual awareness or inner calmness that they themselves aspire to. This, too, is a practice akin to devotion.

Yet it is important to remember that there is no substitute in yoga for the effort of the individual. Devotion also requires our effort; we must nurture it, embody it, envision it, and embrace it. No lasting transformation happens without the active participation of the person being transformed.

You could say that devotion to transformation is required, but devotion to the Divine is up to you!

LET'S DO BOTH

Two little boys were in danger of being late to the school.

"Let us stop and pray for God to get us there on time," said one.

"No, better than that," said the other, "let us run with all our might and pray while we are running."

<hr>

Some Tradition, Little Lineage

The emphasis on traditions and lineages in modern yoga is often an unnecessary distraction to useful practice. It has played a role in yoga becoming factionalized and students occupied with searching for the so-called right tradition or right lineage.

It also creates the impression that there are various conflicting methodologies within yoga.

In fact, there is only one root method: updating our minds and bodies, our mental and physical software, through the eight limbs of yoga.

Sometimes, yoga "traditions" are just exalted terms for brands and labels. The security these labels confer can play us false.

<hr>

RELIGIOUS GAME

A football game was on between the two local football teams. As one team scored, one spectator cheered and threw his hat high in the air. When the other team scored, he was equally delighted.

A puzzled man in the next seat asked, "Which side are you rooting for, my good man?"

"Who, me?" came the reply. "I am not supporting either side. I am just here to enjoy the game."

At which point the questioner turned to a friend next to him, and said, "Hmmph! An atheist."

~~~~~~~~~~

A yoga critic once pointed out to me that some of these traditions have become exclusive yoga clubs that consist of devotees of the method and of a particular teacher associated with it. The wellspring of growth is stifled, resulting in erosion of initiative and dissipation of talent.

Birthright or Choose Right

Our births determine many things about us. Our genes are a big factor in our health and outlook on life, both physical and mental. Beyond that, the circumstances of our lives also dictate our paths, to a point. Our subconscious minds, with the latent impression of all our past actions and experiences (*samskaras,* as they are known in Sanskrit), bring forth reactions to all situations. We feel and think even without knowing it! On one hand, it seems that much of life is not in our hands.

But there is free will and choice.

We can decide to think, feel, and act differently. Instead of reacting to life without awareness, we can choose to respond with care and wisdom. That is the root of personal transformation. That is the root of yoga.

We can effect no real or lasting transformation without this stream of awareness interposed between situation and reaction.

This conscious effort is the basis of yoga. It is this effort that brings about the changes all the way from a distracted mind to complete focus or *samadhi*.

Though a certain capacity for concentration or calmness can be inherited, as can their opposites, it is fundamentally the effort of the individual that determines his progress on the yoga path. The sons of saints can be sinners, and the daughters of sinners can be saints; history bears ample testimony to this fact. Thus yoga is not inherited; it is passed on not from guru to child, but from guru to seeker.

Discipline and wisdom in practice determine the quality of the disciple and his progress in yoga, not merely an accident of birth.

Transformation is not a birthright. It has to be earned. In the nation of transformation, there are no citizens by birth. We are all travelers.

All Paths Lead to One Road

You have no doubt heard the saying, "There are many paths to the top of the mountain." That metaphor is true when speaking of yoga, but with a caveat. There may be many paths, but there is only one main road that all paths join: the eight limbs of yoga.

The Bhagavad Gita has eighteen chapters, which seem to speak of different yogas. At the very least, it is conventional to separate the message of the Bhagavad Gita into three yoga paths: action, devotion, and wisdom. But all these three paths are there in the Yogasutra. It is just the emphasis on certain practices, depending on the stage of the practitioner, that is different.

The foundational practice that combines all these three pathways is called *kriya yoga* in the Yogasutra. Because the mind is restless, we must do something most of the time. Extended stillness is not a realistic option for most of us. Thus the word *kriya*, meaning "action." Three practices or actions are suggested in the Yogasutra as the basis for transformation. Like removing a thorn with a thorn, we use action to bring the mind to stillness.

One is willpower to overcome resistance to transformation. After all, we all experience resistance when we work toward any transformation. Second is self-reflection and wisdom, which we can support with mantra meditation. Third is the attitude of letting go of what we cannot control, for not everything is in our hands.

Thus action, wisdom, and letting go come together in a single foundational path in the Yogasutra.

All three are necessary for everyone, just perhaps one a little more and the other a little less from time to time, depending on the flux of life and the mind.

Householder or monk, everyone does these three practices. The monk does them full time. The householder does them as much as possible! The difference is only in intensity and environment, not in the nature of the practice itself.

Thus there is only one yoga: the yoga of Patanjali.

Roots of the Yoga Path

Yoga has come a long way from its ancient roots. The milieu in which we practice nowadays is vastly different from that of a thousand years ago. In the olden days, the yogi was practicing alone. Now people practice in groups. Yoga was mostly about meditation and pranayama. Now it is mostly about asana. There was little in the way of props then. Now there is a plethora of props to assist us.

This transition has largely been due to the expansion of yoga.

What was a solitary practice of a very few individuals has become a mass movement. This carries with it the seeds of great positive potential.

But to use this moment wisely, we must reflect as we carry this shift forward, blending the best of ancient wisdom with modern progress.

3 *Thinking It Through*

Rethinking

Imagine that you are at the immigration counter at an airport, entering a foreign country. The immigration form will have several questions, such as "What is the purpose of your visit? What is your occupation? Who is your contact person? Where will you be staying?"

Such questions are rational and necessary. We should ask similar questions about any subject we study and any activities that we do over time.

By this inquiry, we determine the following: Is this knowledge or activity useful to me? Is it healthful or harmful? How can I engage in it effectively? What should I do or not do?

It is these questions that we explore in different contexts throughout this book.

What Is Its Nature?

What is the nature of an object or subject? Many qualities and functions go into anything in the world. Generally, we consider that the nature of an object or subject is determined by qualities that are specific to it. A yoga pose, for instance, has specific movements and positioning that are characteristic of it. A particular pranayama has breathing patterns that define it. A branch of mathematics has equations that are specific to it.

The clearer we are about the specific qualities or nature of a subject or method, the more effective we are at understanding it or applying it.

Why Should I?

No one acts without a purpose. The classical purpose of asana, for example, is to reduce the restlessness of the mind and bring lightness to the body.

Being clear about the purpose of the various practices of yoga is important to get the benefits that we really need. On the other hand, purpose should be related to need.

I should do what gives me what I need, not fashion a purpose around a whim! Hence clarity of purpose relates not only to technique but also to self-awareness.

Where Are Its Roots?

What is the origin of a subject, concept, or even a person? For instance, we say, "Victoria is Mary's daughter." We ask, "Which university did he study at?"

Why do we want to know this information? With it, we are able to take a reasoned guess about the nature of the object, subject, or person.

If knowledge or practices arise from roots that are well researched and widespread, they are likely to be more useful and sound.

Similarly, if the origin of an idea is well supported in ancient texts, that fact tells us that the idea may have greater validity. If the origin of an idea is the experience of a single individual, or only my own experience, I should probably view that idea with more care.

What Are Its Connections?

How is the subject under scrutiny connected to other subjects? How is it connected to me? Connections are the basis of relationships between everything: ideas, people, and objects. To know how A influences B, we must know the connection between them.

For instance, to practice pranayama effectively, we must consider that the breath is contained in the body. Thus the movement of the body will necessarily change the breath; if we understand that connection well, we can use it to develop the breath. If we don't understand it, that connection can work against us.

Connections are the basis of relationships in the world too. Our lives are shaped by our connections with people and situations.

Cause and Effect

Ancient Indian logic makes the straightforward postulate that there is no effect without a cause. There may be occurrences whose causes we are unable to learn, but a cause must still exist in reality even if we do not see it. However, there is a difference between proximal and distal causes.

Proximal causes contribute directly or immediately to the outcome. Distal causes contribute indirectly or through a chain of events.

For example, the origin of the universe is the distal cause for everything, but that information has no practical use in daily life. The immediate cause of a fire is a spark or kindling, but other distal causes, past conditions, also contribute to the flame: the wood comes from a tree, the tree must be exposed to dry weather, and so on!

In the context of yoga, for example, practicing calmness or forgiveness may be a direct antidote to anger. Going for a run might be a supportive cause.

Running can help dissipate the bodily energy of anger, and set the platform to reconsider the anger in the mind. But without actively bringing the mind to calmness or forgiveness, running alone is not likely to remove the anger in the long run, as it is only a supportive cause for removing anger.

Considering the difference and nature of proximal and distal causes helps us to be much more effective in the practices we do and the choices we make.

The Donkey Is the Cause

The much-loved example in classical texts to analyze cause and effects is an earthen pot. To come into existence, an earthen pot requires mud, a potter's wheel, and a potter.

The most intimate and direct cause of the pot is the mud. Without mud, the pot is impossible under any circumstances. Among the other two causes, the potter is the causal agent, and the wheel is the support. They are one step removed from the mud in the chain of causation—essential, but not intrinsic to the pot.

What about the donkey that carried the mud for the potter? The donkey is an optional or secondary cause. After all, the mud could be transported in many ways, the donkey being just one.

In other words, hiding the donkey will not stop the potter from making pots; he might just carry some mud himself. Hiding the wheel requires him to get another wheel. Removing the mud makes the pot impossible until more mud is acquired.

To ensure health of mind and body effectively, we must emphasize causes that are proximal before the ones that are distal.

There are proximal and distal causes in any yoga practice, too. In a yoga class, what made you feel well? Was it the teacher? The specific instructions? The asanas themselves? The specific movements? Or was it the breathing, or just the time-out from normal life?

Usually, it is a combination of the above. You don't have to sit down and analyze all of these causes before you practice yoga. But keep an eye on these as separate causes rather than as an

The donkey is the cause!

indivisible entity that is "the practice." Sometimes one of these causes is taking away from rather than contributing to our well-being, and the sooner we recognize that, the more quickly and effectively we can fix it and improve our practice.

"Krishnamacharya Is the Cause of My Back Injury!"

"Krishnamacharya is the cause of my back injury!" said a student to me once. I asked him how that could be, for my teacher, Krishnamacharya, had passed away years before this student started practicing yoga. The student replied, "But my teacher studied in the lineage of Krishnamacharya!"

Krishnamacharya was perhaps four generations of teachers removed from this student. What Krishnamacharya taught had been filtered through many layers, multiple voices, numerous bodies, and varied experiences before it reached this student. Along the way, the key principle Krishnamacharya espoused—that the teaching should be appropriate for the student—was evidently lost. How can Krishnamacharya be responsible for what people did not understand and the distortions they introduced, most after his demise at that? The proximal or direct cause of this student's injury was his yoga teacher and his own practice!

So I said in a lighter vein to the student, "It is not Krishnamacharya but your teacher's car that is the cause of your back injury. If he did not have the car, he would not be able to reach the yoga studio to teach you."

Then I did suggest some changes to his practice, particularly in how he was relating to his breath and body, and also recommended that he find a teacher who was willing to acknowledge the individuality of his body. In other words, I aimed at changing the most proximal causes contributing to the problem.

~~~~~~~~~~

INCORRECT INFERENCE

Child: "Why doesn't daddy have hair on his head?"

Mother: "Daddy thinks a great deal, dear."

Child: "But mummy, why do you have so much hair on your head?"

Mother: "Hush! Eat your breakfast!"

~~~~~~~~~~

Inference

We determine causes and correlations by inference. That inference can be defective. "God is blind," said a person, "because God is love and love is blind!"

For instance, consider the statement "*Pitta* people get angry."

Is that really true? Do people of a *pitta*-dominant constitution actually get more angry than those of a *vata*- or *kapha*-dominant constitution?

Anger is a fundamental emotion, an expression of displeasure with circumstances.

~~~~~~~~~~

ANGER MANAGEMENT

The father saw his son sitting on top of another boy in the front yard.

"Why are you pinning George to the ground like that?" Jimmy's dad demanded.

"He hit me in the eye."

"How many times," reprimanded the father, "have I told you to count up to a hundred before you lose your temper?"

"I am counting to a hundred," Jimmy replied, "but I am sitting on him so he'll be here when I get through counting."

~~~~~~~~~~

People of all constitutional types experience the fundamental emotions of desire and dislike, fear and anger. But how these emotions are propagated and supported in the complex of the body and mind is related to their constitution.

For instance, a person of *vata* constitution might gesticulate more, stride around the room, and speak a lot when she is angry. A person of *pitta* constitution might grit his teeth and speak bitingly, head thrust forward. A person of *kapha* constitution might be slow to acknowledge the displeasure within but hold on to the emotion longer in both body and mind. The same circumstances might provoke displeasure and hence anger in all of them. It is how their body and mind react to this basal emotion that is different.

In both Ayurveda and yoga, it is possible to be misled by inferences that seem superficially correct but, on further analysis, prove to be misleading!

Ancient Logic

Logic is the process by which we determine what is correct and incorrect. The ancient Indian texts also teach the process of logic, calling it *nyaya* or *tarka*.

The thrust of classical Indian logic is that inference is often a clearer guide to certain and accurate knowledge than hearsay and books, or even direct perception. Hearsay and direct perception can be flawed and difficult to correct; inference can be corrected more easily.

A famous quotation goes, "Accept that which is correct by inference, even if said by a child or by a parrot."

That is, do not judge a subject or statement just by who says it; analyze the content that lies behind it and decide for yourself.

Look at the person through the content rather than the content through the person!

Some of what yoga describes are states of mind that are entirely internal, beyond the senses. It is not possible to understand them or the practices that lead to them without inference or logic.

HOW IS IT POSSIBLE?

Question: Two men came out of the chimney. One was dirty in his clothes, and the other was clean. Who will take a bath?

Answer: How can two people come out of the same chimney if one is clean and the other is dirty?

Be Clear, Get Real

As the saying goes, keep an open mind, but not so open that anything comes in and everything goes out! If I accept a teaching on blind faith alone or because the teacher seems authoritative or charismatic, my learning is of debatable value. It is difficult to derive sustainable benefit from a practice that we don't understand or that we misunderstand. I also cannot be certain it will meet my needs and requirements as an individual.

To be clear and get real in any field requires approaching it with an open and inquiring but discerning mind.

Before acting on any information, including yoga teachings, it is wise to ask ourselves

- Is the information sensible? Is it reasonable? Can I verify it to some extent through my own experience?

- Am I carrying my critical-thinking skills into the yoga room?

Belief is not always a good substitute for right knowledge and practice!

- Am I following the teacher's directions with reasonable comprehension of what I am doing and why I am doing it?

- Am I learning invocations, chants, and mantras and knowing their origin or purpose?

- Am I moving my body into pain or practicing in a spirit of competitiveness?

Why Am I Doing Yoga?

The simple answer to this question is that people practice yoga because it helps them in some way. This is as good an answer as any.

That said, any reason is good enough for a while, but good reasons are necessary if the practice is to be useful for a long while!

A yoga practice is unlikely to deliver sustainable benefits unless the reasons why we are practicing yoga are wise reasons.

Here are some reasons why I might practice yoga:

- I am stressed out, and I need a break from the other activities of my life.

- Yoga helps me feel good, at least temporarily.

- I enjoy the challenge of doing more advanced asanas.

- Yoga is mystic, and I find that alluring.

- I need a quick fix because I have little time on my hands.

- I want to give my mind a rest and follow along with the instructions for a while.

None of these reasons is inherently wrong or bad. But they are incomplete or insufficient in themselves.

A yoga class can relieve stress, but we have to look at life itself and mind our minds in daily life activities if we wish to reduce our stress over time.

Yoga is meant to help us feel good. But not all activities and practices that feel good necessarily transform us positively.

The challenge of doing asanas can motivate us to develop strength and flexibility and feel well. Yet it can become a source of injuries and imbalance, too, particularly if it is based on unhealthy competition and ego.

The way out of trouble in asana practice is never as simple as the way in!

The philosophy and psychology of yoga has many layers; its depths can be enticing in what they reveal about life and the mind. But the study of yoga aims not to mystify but to enlighten.

Quick practices that help boost or support the body and mind are very useful. However, shortcuts come with their own caveats.

Short practices yield most benefit in the background of structured, long-term transformational work. But practices that lack depth should not be compensated in length!

It is certainly pleasant to give the mind rest and just move the body, listening to instructions for an hour. Yet, in the long run, that cannot be the only mode of practice we encourage. We have to be present in the moment, experiencing the body and mind, and take responsibility and an active interest in moving and breathing in a way that is tailored for our own needs.

A generic instruction set that accommodates dozens of people cannot be as effective as one's own personal practice.

We can check our shoes at the door of the yoga room, but we have to carry our monkey minds and restless bodies in with us! When we exit the yoga class, we slip into our shoes again, and over the next hour, we also slip into our old minds and bodies. The yoga class may take a couple of our hours of our week, but our minds and bodies are being constantly molded by the rest of the hundred-plus hours.

Being wise and mindful in our yoga practice, and inquiring of how that yoga is helping us, is an essential ingredient in putting yoga to work for our bodies and minds.

Essential, Important, Nice

If life was always about priorities, modern life is about urgent priorities! No one has endless time or energy. Resources are always limited. In the pursuit of yoga, we must expend our resources wisely. We must spend our time doing things that are likely to give us the best return for the time, money, and effort that we invest in them. This is, of course, a general principle in life, and yoga is no exception.

Yoga knowledge and practice can be grouped under three headings along these lines: the essential, the important, and the nice.

Focus first on the essential, and then on the important, and lastly on the nice.

Example 1

Essential to Know

The goal of the all classical yoga practice is to bring about a state of calm clarity, balanced energy, and lightness of body and mind (*satva*). To do this, a concomitant reduction of restless (*rajas*) and dullness (*tamas*) is necessary. This is the central thread of asana practice as well. An asana practice that does not achieve this is likely to stagnate over a couple of years and can also have adverse physical and psychological consequences (witness the yoga injuries and body image problems that beset current day yoga).

Important to Know

Some classical texts say there are as many asanas as there are living beings in the world. Other texts say there are 8.4 million asanas, or 84,000. The point is that classical asanas are not in themselves sacrosanct. There can be innumerable variations.

Nice to Know

Asana is a gender-neutral word.

The Sanskrit names of asanas are also interesting but nonessential information.

Example 2

Essential to Know

Headstand is a mudra in classical yoga texts. It is not just the posture of being upside down but rather the combination of deep breathing and the bandhas in the posture, with inward focus, that delivers the complete benefits of the asana.

The downward facing dog is an important asana because it helps prepare for the bandhas.

Important to Know

The method of practicing the bandhas in the downward facing dog and in headstand, and how the spine and breathing should be in these asanas, is important.

Nice to Know

Headstand is also called *kapalasana* or *brahmarandrasana* because we rest on the crown of the head.

Possible, Distant, Ultimate

Any endeavor in life is undertaken with some outcome in mind. Consciously, we may not be entirely clear of what that desired outcome is, but there is a drive within us, at least subconsciously that impels us. Being unclear of what we wish to achieve is a recipe for incoherent action, a meandering journey, and an uncertain result.

Is it a good idea to enroll in university or start a business, unclear of the milestones along the path—without knowing where we expect to see ourselves every six months or every year down the line? No. A good university tries to help students do this for themselves at every step.

Yoga practice is not an exception to this general rule in life. Yoga is an ancient practice and a long path; we had better be clear of the milestones along the way. In other words, it is wise to first consider what is possible and what is not.

Mistaking the practically impossible for the realistically achievable is a recipe for pointless pursuit.

Three words are useful here: ultimate, distant, and possible.

The ultimate goal of classical yoga is complete stillness of the mind, but this is achievable only for the occasional rare soul. A distant goal for many yoga practitioners could be to sit in meditation for a couple of hours. Goals in the near term that are actually possible include increased strength and flexibility in the body, lightness and clarity of the mind, a sense of well-being and calm, more impulse control, etc.

The goalposts are different for each individual, and they're moving all the time.

As our practice ebbs and flows, so do the goals. It is imperative to be aware of what those goals are, how relevant they are, and how far away they are.

~~~~~~~~~~

TOO MUCH CHANGE

A girl asked her boyfriend on the eve of marriage, "If we get married, will you give up smoking?"

"Yes, dear."

"And drinking, too?"

"Yes, dear."

"And will you stop going to your club in the evening?"

"Yes."

"And what else are you thinking of giving up, darling?"

"The idea of getting married."

~~~~~~~~~~

4 *From Body Inward*

The Feel-Good Factor

Yoga is a pathway to positive changes in body and mind. But most people practice yoga not because they have a specific transformation in mind but simply because yoga makes them feel good.

Not all positive change in life necessarily feels good at the outset.

We all know this. Quitting smoking or exercising more every day doesn't always feel good; it is a challenge, and we have to push ourselves to do it. But the outcome is beneficial; we do experience a more positive state of body and mind afterward.

Yoga acknowledges this resistance to change as a fundamental barrier to positive transformation.

The Yogasutra calls the persistence we need to overcome that resistance *tapas*.

But where is the line between a practice that merely feels good and one that creates truly beneficial change over time?

As I noted earlier, not every activity that feels good leads us to a better state of body and mind in time. But the converse is not true either—activities that feel bad don't necessarily lead to positive transformation. In fact, what feels bad to the body and mind is actually harmful most of the time.

We must be clear why we are moving around in asanas: we praise the bee and swat the mosquito!

We know that people can indulge in self-destructive behavior because it feels good at some level to them. Many addictions fall under this category.

Can we be addicted to asana or other practices of yoga? Can a person do yoga practices because he feels good even if they aren't really helping him in the long term?

Unfortunately, yes. And you have probably come across people who are in this trap.

For most people, asana starts as a powerfully transformative practice for their bodies, and partly their minds. In time, typically, progress slows down, and even regression is possible. This is because of the nature of body and mind.

Asana practice should not become a struggle. Instead, there should be harmony between the breath and the body.

The three *gunas*, clarity and lightness (*satva*), activity and restlessness (*rajas*), and subsiding and dullness (*tamas*), are in constant flux. Feeling good is usually a consequence of rotation among these.

In particular, neither *rajas* nor *tamas* feels good over an extended time; our body and mind begin to wish for the opposite to restore balance. When we feel very dull, activity can help us feel good. Conversely, when we feel restless and disturbed, slowing down and resting helps us feel better. Neither sleep and rest nor activity and engagement make us feel good after some time. We need the rotation among the modes of activity and rest.

This is like receiving a massage. Within limits, a massage feels good, but if it continues for hours, it begins to induce pain rather than pleasure!

Positive transformation, in contrast to feeling good, requires more than just rotating between the flux of modes in the mind and body.

Lasting positive change in body and mind arises from shifting the base mode of the mind and body toward *satva*—lightness in the body and clarity in the senses and mind.

As an automatic consequence, the practice also feels good, as the body and mind stay steady in a positive state for longer periods of time.

The *Hatha Yoga Pradipika* explains what to expect from an asana practice.

Carrot stock is in surplus. If we stick to the plan
now, our profits will multiply for sure.

Carrot stock is in surplus. If we multiply as
planned now, the world is ours for sure.

A MATTER OF PERSPECTIVE

"Slimness of the body, pleasantness on the face,

clarity in the voice, and luster in the eyes,

freedom from disease, and metabolism kindled well,

mind focused inward, and the nadis pure,

these are the signs of success in the hatha yoga path."

You may note the repetitive theme of lightness of the body and clarity at gross and subtle levels. Thus classical hatha yoga is meant to gradually turn us toward that quality of *satva* or, in other words, to bring about real and lasting transformation.

It is possible to practice asanas differently from this ideal, though. If the principal barometer is feeling good rather than positive transformation, injuries can result from asana practice. That's because feeling good is not judged by the body alone but by the mind as well—sometimes mainly by the mind.

If my mind will be satisfied and feel good only when my head is on my knees with my legs straight, I may end up hurting my back to get there.

I am sure many readers will agree from their own experience that this mind-set is not all that uncommon in the gym or in an asana class.

When done this way—without monitoring our inner compulsions or minding our minds—asana can become a habit.

There are no more useful updates to the body and mind! An unconscious habit cannot bring about constructive changes in body-mind patterns. Habits can only reinforce existing patterns. Only conscious effort can create change.

In a yoga practice where feeling good is the guide, the goals we set for ourselves may not be truly the ones that will lead us to a better place in time. What feels good to us can fluctuate, as the tendency toward restless and dullness (*rajas* and *tamas*) in our body and mind ebbs or rises.

For instance, many people with back pain try to stretch their aching muscles, maybe in a yoga class, to relieve the pain. It feels better temporarily, only to return in a few hours. The underlying problem could be that their muscles might be not only tight or overworked but also weak. To relieve their pain, they might need judicious strengthening rather than stretching.

But strengthening may not feel good right away; it may not appear to be helping immediately. Give the regimen some days to weeks, though, and the back pain might be substantially alleviated. In this case, what felt good (stretching) was not the practice (strengthening) that could bring about the positive change (freedom from back pain)!

To ensure that our practice is relevant to us, we must ensure that we stay mindful of the goal.

Not only should the practice feel good, it must also lead us toward a more balanced and posi-

tive state of body and mind, one of lightness and clarity.

Once this goal is clear to us, we have to be mindful of the body and mind, adjust accordingly to address imbalances, and do neither too much nor too little, avoiding both compulsion and indolence. The way to do this is by working with the body and the breath.

Moving the body reduces heaviness and dullness, or diminishes tamas. Comfortably long and smooth breathing reduces the restlessness in the body and mind, or diminishes rajas.

By doing both in asana, we encourage a lighter and clearer state of mind and body (*satva*).

As this state of mind emerges, we endeavor to deepen and extend it as the foundation for deeper practices of pranayama and meditation, and as the support for a healthy body and calm mind. This is the basis of an asana practice for positive transformation rather than only feeling good in the moment.

The real art of creating a right practice is not only to include the right postures in the right place, but to leave the wrong ones out.

OTHERWISE GOOD

In a seminar, I once came across a student suffering from pain in his shoulder. His daily asana practice would sometimes aggravate the pain so badly that he would have to stop moving and wait until he recovered enough to continue.

I asked him why he didn't just take a break from the asana practice and allow his shoulder some time to recover.

He replied that while the asana practice hurt his shoulder, it made him feel good otherwise!

Self-Practice or Group Practice?

Yoga is something you do for yourself. No one else can do it for you, nor can you do it for someone else. In essence, it is an intensely individual pursuit. To this, add the fact that no one person is exactly like another in body and mind, and you see why classical yoga was always self-practice done by individuals.

However, the format of yoga is quite different now. It is not practiced in the caves of the Himalayas but in well-equipped yoga studios across the world. And it is practiced not alone, but as a group.

There are reasons practicing yoga in a group is helpful. The energy of the group can support you and add to your motivation. Listening to the teacher guide you through the practice means you can stop thinking about what you should be doing for that one hour. You can network with a community of like-minded students.

But there are important reasons why you should also practice yoga in your own time and space.

Motivation is key to transformation, and even if it is for a short time a day, stepping on to the mat and sustaining that motivation by yourself can help you discipline your wandering mind very effectively. Rather than handing your motivation to the group, develop the willpower to do it on your own.

Practicing at your own pace allows you to appreciate your breath and body better and to explore and expand your awareness. A flow of instructions from a teacher allows you to tune out and just follow along, diminishing your own alertness and presence in the practice.

You are like no other individual; every person is different in countless ways in body and mind. Unless you do your yoga practice on your own, you will never have the possibility of a practice that truly supports the needs of your body and mind. Further, it is only your own practice that can evolve intelligently with time and effort to suit you best. Everyone in a group cannot evolve at the same pace or in the same way.

Finally, the deeper aspects of yoga—mudras, pranayama, and meditation—cannot be explored by synchronizing your practice with a dozen others in a group. You can access these practices only by deepening your inner awareness in your practice. A group cannot help you here; it can only be a distraction.

I am not advising that you drop out of group classes altogether. Rather, I recommend that you work toward developing your personal self-practice as the main course of your yoga meal and the group practice as the garnishing that you add for taste. Only in your self-practice will you find the real depth of yoga.

Tenacious, Not Torturous

Anything worth achieving requires commitment and effort. And along the way, we will face challenges and resistance to change. Yoga is no different.

When we set out to transform our minds and bodies through yoga, it is not always a stroll in a garden of roses! The journey is more like a hike across unfamiliar country where beauty coexists with hurdles like thorny bushes, steep hills, and deep rivers across our path.

> *To change our bodies and minds for the better, we may need to overcome resistance from the body and even more from the mind.*

If we give up whenever we encounter a challenge because it is too uncomfortable to face, we will never make any progress. Our bodies and minds will remain stuck in their old patterns.

This persistence in the face of discomfort and challenge is called *tapas* in the Yogasutra. Quite literally, the word *tapas* derives from the root words "to heat," and "to bear mental discomfort." Facing challenges is a tough business, and enough to make us sweat, metaphorically!

But *tapas* is not literally sweating out toxins; the idea is not that the hotter the yoga class, the more the *tapas*! It does not have to do with external heat or removing physical toxins from the body; that should happen naturally by asana and pranayama practice.

As Vyasa, the preeminent commentator on the Yogasutra, says, pushing the body to extremes is rarely beneficial in bringing balance to the mind. He points out that moderate fasting can be very helpful in disciplining the body and mind, but an extreme diet is not *tapas*. Instead, it is a pathway to upset the health of the body and calmness of the mind. That cannot be *tapas*, for it would be contrary to the central thread of yoga: well-being of the body and mind.

The concept of tapas is to burn the past tendencies that drag us back to our old ways, both in body and mind, in the metaphorical fire of steadfast commitment to the practice.

The intention is to create a positive transformation in the *mind*, not just in the body. In short, *tapas* is to melt away our resistance and negative tendencies by sustaining our yoga practice in the face of challenges, but maintaining such persistence only to the point where it is actually helping our mind and body.

When the yoga practitioner has the tenacity of *tapas*, she is able to stay steady in her practice regardless of the ups and downs of life.

Neither Ideal Body nor Idle Body

Classical yoga tells us that we are the awareness within, not the clothes that wrap our bodies, the bodies that hold our senses, the senses that serve our mind, or even our minds themselves. That is a deep message, indeed.

But the messages we receive nowadays are unfortunately at the other end of the spectrum. Weight-loss-obsessed, I-am-my-body culture is pervasive, in yoga too. Nourishing the body for health, appreciating the enjoyment it brings, and cherishing it for our future years—these are all good. But the exaggerated pursuit of glorifying the body adds very little meaning to lives.

Authentic yoga has nothing against the body because without a healthy body it is very difficult to have a calm mind. But an ideal body and an ideal yoga pose are trite goals; there are wiser and more lasting life goals we could be pursuing through the practice of yoga. Consequently, the practice of asanas in yoga is not an end in itself. Asana is a means to positive transformation in the body and mind. Its goal is to bring lightness and brightness into body and mind and, ultimately, into every aspect of our lives.

Many people—even in India—are surprised to learn that yoga has more to do with the mind than with the body. Yoga is an intelligent approach to balance, quietness, and peace of mind so that we can think more clearly and act more positively and effectively. It is primarily an internal rather than external practice.

Or, to put it another way, yoga is a "work-in" within a workout.

The practice of asanas—the physical postures of yoga—is but one aspect of the practice of yoga. If mastering yoga postures is the primary goal of our yoga practice, we are like the man in the following story.

~~~~~~~~~~

WHAT AM I CHASING?

A nearsighted man lost his hat in a strong wind. He began chasing the hat but could never quite catch it. A woman from a nearby farmhouse called out to the man, "What are you doing?!"

The man replied that he was trying to retrieve his hat. "Your hat, sir, is on the other side of that stone wall," shouted the woman. "What you have been chasing is my little black hen!"

~~~~~~~~~~

Yoga Cake

Many equate the term yoga with stretching, for that's what they do in their yoga classes: they bend and stretch their bodies into various positions.

But we just cannot bend and stretch ourselves into a life transformation, which is the real goal of yoga. Life transformation occurs in the context of how we relate to our own lives and the people and situations in it.

Without a transformative goal, yoga classes can become what might be better called asana-stics or asana-bics like gymnastics or aerobics rather than the asana of classical yoga.

If the focus in asana is solely on achievement, alignment, and adjustment but not greater health and well-being, we must ask ourselves whether it is really yoga practice.

For the practice of asana is not just the physical act of the postures but also using them to progress toward a calm mind within. And this can happen only if we cultivate mindful awareness of the body, discrimination on what is healthy, and balanced reflection on the bigger picture in the asana practice itself.

There is nothing inherently wrong with any asana practice technique, be it one of alignment or hands-on work, so long as it is done safely and with one eye on the student and the other eye on the greater goal of bringing well-being to the body and mind. The problem arises when these techniques are applied blindly as an end in themselves, to serve the system or style, or for the benefit of the teacher or the ego of the student.

Asanas are part of a bigger picture. Extracting asanas from the systematic and progressive practice of yoga and calling them yoga is akin to holding up two eggs and calling them cake.

Eggs and flour! Bake it on your own!

Asanas, like eggs, can be good in and of themselves. But to mistake the part for the whole is unwholesome for our well-being!

That Perfect Posture

Mastery in asana practice, according to Krishnamacharya, was the ability to remain in a particular asana with long, smooth breathing.

Krishnamacharya used to say, "External alignment relies more on the body, while internal alignment relies more on the breath."

Alignment is fundamentally individual. Alignment is not in reference to an external ideal but to the relationship of the body parts to one another, both inside and out. Traditionally, this was expressed as the distance between particular points on the *nadis* or the *cakras*, and that distance was individualized based on finger width.

In any asana we are working with alignment at both gross and subtle levels. The more gross alignment is amenable to easy visual examination and correction through musculoskeletal re-alignments. Internal alignment is better judged by feeling the flow of the breath and subtle inner sensations of the body.

Further, in an asana practice, precise external alignment is not as important as the deeper sensations of the inner body and the flow of the breath. We must have a feeling of well-being during the practice.

The goal is a present awareness and inner attention rather than perfect mastery of the external form.

A student who strains to touch her forehead to her knees in a seated forward bend while ignoring the feeling of the asana within and how it impacts the breath, the prana, and the mind is cultivating an unquiet state of being rather than doing yoga.

A proper asana practice brings about lightness of body and brightness of mind. It reduces our mental and physical hyperactivity and instills a sense of calmness from the beginning to the end of the practice. This can be done even when practicing more challenging asanas. That synergy of the inner and outer experience leading us toward well-being, not the form of the posture, is the hallmark of the ideal asana.

Yoga Flow

A vinyasa, as commonly understood, consists of moving from one asana or body position to another, combining breathing with the movement. This is a word popularized by Krishnamacharya in his teachings and has become part of the yoga lexicon.

The deeper import of the word vinyasa is to place things where they belong or are appropriate.

The concept is to take orderly steps, each step placed correctly, while considering the person and goal so that progress is consistent and steady.

A microcosm of vinyasa is a flow of asanas where each asana is a step to the next. The concept as envisioned by Krishnamacharya is meant to have a much wider scope and depth, however. That is why he used to say, "Do not practice asanas and other disciplines without vinyasa (orderly steps)."

The concept of vinyasa applies not only to the body but to the breath, senses, and mind as well. Without progressive steps in deepening mental focus, there is no vinyasa at the mental level in asana practice. Since yoga is itself about bringing the mind to stillness, vinyasa necessarily implies orderly steps toward a steady mind.

Thus vinyasa in asana practice should also incorporate minding the mind in a progressive manner.

As Krishnamacharya once elaborated, "Do not practice asana, pranayama, meditation, vedic chanting, dance, without *vrtti nirodha* or mental focus. Practice all of them in orderly steps."

THEORY AND ACTION

The young preacher thrilled his congregation with his first sermon, a challenge to "gird their loins" for Christian service and living. Then, to their dismay, he preached the same sermon the following Sunday. When he confronted them with the same message on the third Sunday, his flock felt something must be done.

"Don't you have more than one sermon?" blurted a spokesman to the pastor.

"Oh, yes," he answered quietly, "I have quite a number of sermons. But you have not done anything about the first one yet."

As Fast as You Can

Krishnamacharya was once asked in an interview, "Should yoga practice be done fast, and why or why not?" He replied, "Fast movements will distort both the blood circulation and the respiration. This results in crookedness of the body and injury to the different parts of the body. Slow practice of asanas with proper respiration will not only remove the defects in the body but result in *citta ekagrata* (focus of the mind). However, I must insist that this practice should be done from the direct instruction of a teacher."

Do as Much as You Can

Asana practice should be such that we are inspired and challenged to do more. However, there is always that little detail in life known as balance! "Do as much as you can" is good advice only for some students.

Some students will do too little. And some will do far too much. Helping the student find that middle ground where there is sufficient challenge to ensure progress but not enough to cause frustration and injury—that is the responsibility of the teacher.

In the setting of group classes today, where we have many students and one teacher, this responsibility becomes all the more relevant.

Without oversight, students often learn the technique but not the approach.

The teacher must convey not only method but a healthy attitude as well. Teaching is easy when you don't know, but hard when you do!

There is a systematic way to prepare for a difficult asana and to balance the stresses of the body after doing it. The teacher must have that knowledge and adapt it to the student within the constraints of the class.

Without adequate instruction and suitable perspective, the instruction "do as much as you can" may have deceptive consequences!

Miracles, by definition, occur very rarely.

AS MUCH AS YOU CAN

A judge sentenced a dangerous criminal on twenty-two counts, to serve a term of five years for each offense.

The man in the dock protested, "But that's impossible! It comes to more than a hundred years!"

The judge leaned forward and said quietly, "Don't worry. Just do as much as you can!"

Asana Bites

Yoga is a way of bringing positive changes in our life. Positive change requires opposing past habits. But asanas can also become habits. If we practice asana like riding a bicycle, we lose a large part of its transformative potential.

Movement becomes mechanical because our brain learns movement patterns. If we do a movement some hundreds of times, we can then repeat it easily with little awareness. But awareness is the key to sustaining transformation; awareness helps us recognize what we need to change and prevents us from slipping back after we change.

For asanas to be a powerful agent of transformation, we must do them not purely from the force of habit but with a stream of awareness.

Even for the health of the body—to improve posture and alignment, to increase strength and flexibility effectively, and to explore our limits safely—awareness is necessary in asana practice. Injuries and imbalances in alignment often arise in asana practice because of practicing from habit instead of practicing in awareness.

The best pathway to awareness in asana practice is the connection between the body and breath.

Focusing the mind on the breath, and noticing how the body and breath influence each other, is a profoundly healthful method of developing and maintaining awareness in asana practice.

Look at the word habit. If you remove the *h, a bit* remains. If you remove the *a, bit* of the habit remains. Even when you remove the *b, it* remains! Habits take time to change, and we need to chip away at them bit by bit!

~~~~~~~~~~

ONLY WAY TO DO IT

Two convention delegates, strangers to each other, were sharing a hotel room.

As they were dressing for the formal dinner, one asked the other, "Say, can you tie my tie? My wife always does mine, but she is not along this trip."

"Sure can; lie down flat on the bed," the other said, and he proceeded to do a beautiful job on the tie.

"That's swell," said his roommate, "but tell me, why did I have to lie down on the bed so you could fix my tie?"

"Well, you see," replied the obliging one, "I am an undertaker, and that is the only way I can do it."

~~~~~~~~

Don't Do It

Remember that your own experience trumps the hatha yoga texts. That is, if a practice makes you feel unwell or uncomfortable, it is a good idea to stop it and examine why or if there are alternatives that make you feel better.

While persistence is a virtue, blind adherence is risky.

Consequently, we must learn to differentiate between the healthful discomfort of resistance from past habits and the unhealthful discomfort of trauma and upset to the body or mind. The pathway of yoga is about commitment to positive transformation, not commitment to placing the body and mind in discomfort and harm for no clear reason.

Some people say, "Challenge yourself." But if the mind challenges the body indiscriminately, it may ruin the body.

Some hatha yoga practices can appear weird, such as some forms of the cleansing like swallowing a cloth and removing it; or be unhealthful, like some prolonged fast breathing practices; or be injurious, like forcing oneself into asanas one is not ready for.

It can appear attractive to do some of these things because they are mystic or because the classical texts hard sell them. But it is important to be clear of their benefits when doing them and of their limitations as well as our own.

In short, if you are in doubt, do not persist in doing it. Research, reflect, and then return to the practice, clearer.

~~~~~~~~

DON'T DO IT

There are two butterflies. The male butterfly told the female, "I can bring down this banyan tree by flapping my wings."

A sage was walking by who knew the language of the butterflies. He summoned the male butterfly and said, "You know that you cannot bring down the banyan tree by flapping your wings. Why did you say so?"

The male replied, "I wanted to impress her."

The sage said, "Don't do it!" and dismissed it. When the female asked what the sage had said, the male replied, "Don't do it!"

~~~~~~~~

Now I See It, Now I Want It

Every yoga practice should have a goal and a challenge. However, why is modern yoga dominated almost entirely by postures as goals of practice?

The primary reason is that setting a physical goal is easier than setting a psychological one.

It requires less skill, effort, and time from both teacher and student, and so it is easy to default to it.

Another reason is that a physical goal, like doing a handstand or placing one's head on one's knees, is tangible and easy to appreciate. Psychological goals are harder to appreciate, especially in a group.

The yoga studio setting in which people practice yoga nowadays is also a contributor. Often, numbers are the goal, and students are profit units rather than individuals! Many yoga studios think that the more excitement they can generate, the better for business. In the rush for more students, there is a race to the bottom in skill of teaching and attention to students; often asanas are the only goals that can be taught in such classes. The deeper aspects of yoga require smaller classes, greater skill from the teacher, and patience from the student—and it is not in the commercial interest of many yoga studios to encourage any of these.

But it is not fair to lay the responsibility principally on the studios. They have a business to run, and most small yoga studios struggle to make ends meet and often have sincere teachers.

At a deeper lever, the limitation arises from the expectations of students, which is shaped by the culture of our times.

Life is fast paced. Many of life's goals are material. Competition is encouraged, and ambition is feted. Transplant this mind-set into a yoga class, and each person wants to do the complex asanas that another person is able to do, regardless of whether doing so is wise. The goal of doing some of these asanas seems attractive as it is a visible achievement. Psychological goals are inner achievements whose rewards are not immediately visible, though they are more meaningful in time.

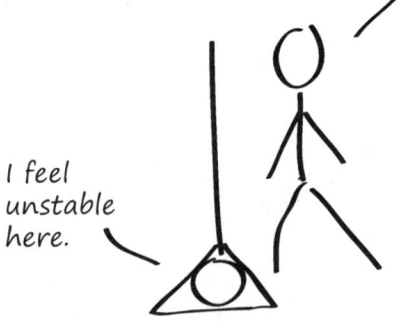

Asana made easy.

The young father pushing a baby carriage seemed quite unperturbed by the wails emerging from it. "Easy now, Albert," he said quietly, "control yourself, keep calm."

Another howl rang out.

"Now, now, Albert," murmured the parent, "keep your temper."

A young mother passing by remarked, "I must congratulate you! You know just how to speak to babies calmly and gently." She patted the youngster on the head and cooed, "What is bothering you, Albert?"

"No, no!" said the father. "His name is Johnny. I am Albert."

Hot, Hotter

Ancient yogis developed the practice of yoga in natural surroundings. They were neither practicing in air-conditioned rooms nor artificially boosting the temperature above normal. Yogis in the Himalayas used asana and breathing techniques to preserve or increase their body heat, but they did not deliberately impose external heat on themselves, at least no more than needed to restore their surroundings to livable temperatures.

Subjecting the body to extreme heat or cold is potentially disturbing to both mind and body, and therefore not recommended in classical yoga practice. Whatever the current practice of hot yoga may be, it is not traditional.

A basic tendency of our bodies is to maintain a state of equilibrium.

When the external temperature changes, our body responds by attempting to restore equilibrium. For example, when the outside temperature is cold, our bodies shiver to retain heat; when the outside temperature is hot, our bodies produce sweat to cool ourselves.

Deliberately introducing temperature extremes puts stress on our body. Doing so while engaging in physical activity compounds the stress. It is important to keep this in mind, especially for people with cardiovascular problems. After all, few of us would choose to walk on a treadmill or do strength training in a room heated to more than one hundred degrees. According to Ayurveda, doing so could disturb the *pitta* in the body.

Yoga Body

A young woman from New Zealand asked whether her brother, who had suffered a high spinal injury and was a quadriplegic, could still practice yoga. He was awake, alert, and could control his breathing. The answer was "Yes, certainly!"

If we think of yoga as being only or mainly asana, we will have difficulty accommodating those with physical limitations.

How can someone with quadriplegia do asanas? However, if we look at the breadth of classical yoga teachings, we see that there is so much that we can do gainfully with the breath and the mind! The young man, despite his limitations, was able to do mindfulness, mantra meditation, pranayama, and several other yoga practices. His condition forced him to look beyond the body, but that is a lesson that all of us would do well to learn.

5 *From Breathing Deeper*

Breathing Is Not Optional

Breathing is the link between body and mind in the yoga practice. In truth, breathing is a foundational link between body and mind, period.

Breathing is an involuntary process that is also partly voluntary. We have no direct control over other involuntary body functions such as digestion, hormone secretions, or our immune system, but we do have a degree of voluntary control over the breath. Furthermore, breathing is a vital life function. This is a unique combination.

Thus breathing is a voluntary doorway to the involuntary body, a conscious doorway to the subconscious mind.

Breathing directly influences the state of body and mind in ways that are not always apparent, at levels that are not always visible on the surface.

Pranayama is the yoga practice of working with the breath. But the breath is ever present as a companion in asana and in meditation. In doing pranayama, it is important to settle both the body and the mind. When the body is still and the mind is settled, we effectively access the subtle experience of the breath. So we should not practice pranayama mechanically. We should pay active attention to steadying the mind and the body before and during the practice.

Yes, Hatha Yoga Is Breathing

The *Hatha Yoga Pradipika's* description of hatha yoga is centered on the practice of pranayama. Hatha yoga is defined as the union of prana and apana. Prana is inhalation; apana is exhalation.

The mind and breath are deeply connected. It is in our experience that disturbed breathing disturbs the mind in turn. Similarly, when our breathing is calm, we can notice that our minds also tend to be calm. For instance, if we are watching a suspenseful scene in a movie, we tend to hold our breath. By controlling the breath, we may control the mind. In pranayama, we attempt this. By slowing down and controlling the breath with attention, we aim to bring focus to the mind.

When we practice such pranayama, it is necessary that we keep the body still, usually seated, thus ensuring the actions of the body are minimized and the senses are not distracted or restless. And when we do such pranayama, we must focus the mind on a steady object of attention.

Through such pranayama, because the prana is restricted from being scattered outside, and by the effort to still our thoughts, the mind gains the nature of being consistently focused.

The ancient text *Yoga Yajnavalkya* describes this. It says the body is ninety-six *angulas* (an ancient measurement) in height from head to toe and in breadth across the outstretched arms. The prana extends twelve *angulas* beyond the body, meaning that the scattering of our attention and energy through body movement, distracted senses, and unfocused mind results in our life force being dissipated. By the practice of pranayama, that scattered prana is contained within the body, meaning that the body is stilled, the senses are drawn in, and the mind is focused.

Touched (with)in the Head

Krishnamacharya used to say, "To cure the ills of the body, use the body. To cure the wandering of the mind, practice pranayama."

Pranayama is also called the yoga of inner touch. The feeling of prana or life force is a subtle inner sensation. Practicing gradually more refined pranayama is a pathway to this experience of prana. The feeling of the breath, as it grows increasingly subtle, can lead us to the experience of the sheath of prana, or the feeling of this life force within us. This is a form of inner sensation, or inner touch.

Hence, pranayama is also sometimes referred to as the yoga of inner touch in classical texts.

This is a key understanding in pranayama practice. This inner touch that we cultivate should be pleasant and easy. As the mind settles onto that feeling, it leads to progressively greater inner awareness, and the senses are drawn inward, away from the distraction that beckon from without. Thus *pratyahara* or sense control becomes easy.

As the sensation of the prana within is pleasant and easy, mental focus on it is not difficult. Thus pranayama becomes a pathway to establish the next two limbs of yoga—sense control and meditation. Among the classical yoga texts, the *Yoga Yajnavalkya* explains this process very well.

Needless to say, if we are to succeed in such pranayama practice, awareness and pleasantness of the breath should be cultivated whenever possible in asana itself. Hence the emphasis on breath focus in asana in Krishnamacharya's teachings.

Ride the Horse

The prana or the breath is like a horse. The mind is the rider.

If the rider does not have a sure touch or is inattentive, the horse may become restless and throw the rider, especially when attempting a more advanced maneuver. So it is with the mind in pranayama.

If I am inattentive, overconfident, or simply lacking in technique, pranayama can create problems. Hence the classical texts caution that the breath must be tamed slowly, like a wild animal.

Like valuable packages in transit, the breath must be stamped "Handle with care!" because the breath can create problems in both body and mind if managed inappropriately.

Physiological problems and mental disturbances can develop over time in those who practice inappropriate and forceful pranayama. People do notice when asana practice causes them

Mondays are the worst, but he's much more tolerable since he started the cooling breath.

"We plan to introduce him to ahimsa next. If he doesn't take to it, there's always the rabbits."

pain or injury. The warning signs are not so apparent when the pranayama they do is harming them. The effect of imbalanced pranayama can be insidious, manifesting as gradual and subtle problems in the body physiology or psychology.

To avoid problems in pranayama practice, here is a simple principle to remember: pranayama begins as just breath awareness, and that quality of breath awareness is part of the practice at all times. That is, we must never lose the awareness of and comfort with the breath in the pranayama practice.

Pranayama: Hoary or Hairy?

The word *loma* in Sanskrit means "hair." This word appears in relation to pranayama: *anuloma* or *viloma* pranayama, for instance. What does hair have to do with pranayama? It is a metaphor, of course; we are not practicing pranayama through our hair! But what does this metaphor indicate?

Look at a strand of hair and notice how thin or subtle it is. Touch a strand of hair and feel how smooth it is. These are the two qualities that the breath should have in the pranayama practice: subtle and smooth.

In fact, these qualities of the breath should be developed in asana practice itself.

The less the strain in an asana, the longer and smoother the breathing should be.

When the breath becomes long and smooth, it serves as the anchor of the yoga practice. It weaves a constant thread through the asana, pranayama, and meditation. A quality of pervasive steadiness underpins a practice supported by a long and smooth breath.

To define pranayama as "breath control" is like defining meditation as "mind control."

Meditation cannot be forced by repressing the thoughts in the mind. Neither can pranayama be forced by trying to control the breath.

The root of pranayama is the subtle experience of the breath. Pranayama is a constantly evolving practice with one eye on the present quality of the breath and the other eye on the place of length and smoothness we wish to guide the breath to.

~~~~~~~~~

DREAMING OF HEAVEN

A man dreamt that he was being carried in the arms of an angel.

In anticipation, he asked breathlessly, "Are you carrying me to heaven? What will I see there?"

The angel replied, "You tell me. It's your dream."

~~~~~~~~~

Breathe: Fast, Faster, Fastest

Fast breathing techniques are rather popular in some styles of yoga nowadays. The classical yoga texts mention two fast breathing exercises: *kapalabhati* and *bhastrika*.

The Yogasutra does not suggest these practices. Fundamentally, these two practices are better considered as cleansing techniques than as pranayama.

Fast breathing is hyperventilation, and physiologically, it can quite easily result in dizziness.

Once I remember a student feeling like this and asking me, "Am I going to heaven?" I told him, "Persist in this practice, and the hospital is where you may go!" Fast breathing should logically be taught for a limited count or duration and interspersed with much greater counts or duration of long and deep breathing. It also needs preparation and balance through asanas, such as the practice of inversions like shoulderstand.

The Ayurvedic constitution of the student also matters.

Fast breathing is more useful in a kapha-dominant condition and often contraindicated in a vata-dominant condition.

In short, fast breathing techniques should not be standardized and handed out to everyone. They should be taught after considering the needs and health of the student. If you are in doubt or do not feel so well after pranayama that incorporates prolonged *kapalabhati* or *bhastrika*, try stopping the fast breathing for a few weeks and see how you feel.

~~~~~~~~~

BE CLEAR WHERE YOU ARE GOING

An absentminded professor got off his train, running an hour late. He rushed out and jumped into a cab, shouting to the driver, "Hurry! Top speed!"

A little later, as they were racing through the streets, he realized he was not sure if he had named his destination. He asked the cabbie, "Did I tell you where I want to go?"

"No, sir," said the cabbie, "but I am driving as fast as I can."

~~~~~~~~~

Five-Star Hotels for Five Senses

Our senses are the gateway to the world outside us. The things we see, hear, smell, taste, and touch leave a mark on our minds. A steady diet of negative television and film images is just as harmful as a steady diet of inappropriate food.

This fact can be difficult to accept in a world that is teeming with sensory information. We can easily become overwhelmed by sights and sounds alone. It is hard to escape flickering televisions, blaring music, and imposing billboards. These create disturbances in our minds, and we become distracted, a word whose literal meaning is "pulled apart."

Excitement of our senses makes our minds subservient to our senses.

~~~~~~~~~~

GOD-GIVEN

The teacher reprimanded a young student for watching a prohibited movie. The student countered, "God has given us eyes to see." The teacher replied, "Yes, but he has also given us eyelids."

~~~~~~~~~~

Managing (not repressing) our senses wisely conserves our energy and liberates our minds.

This aspect of yoga, called *pratyahara*, is the fifth limb of the eight limbs of yoga.

A sage once remarked, "The tongue has two uses—to eat and to talk—and both need to be reduced in half."

~~~~~~~~~~

EATEN BY THE SENSES

A hunter went out with a long-range rifle and came upon a huge bear.

The hunter said to the bear, "I want a fur coat."

The bear said, "I am looking for my breakfast. Why not come to my den and talk it over?"

The hunter and the bear sat down to work out an agreement. After a while the bear got up all alone. They had reached a compromise. The bear got its breakfast, and the hunter had on his fur coat.

~~~~~~~

Developing Your Inner Helpline

Many of us seem to be living as if we are under siege. We exist in a matrix of anxiety, tension, pressure, unease, and confusion. Our lives are marked more by doing than being. We attribute this state to the demands of modern life, but this reasoning carries the suggestion of a kind of helplessness. We can all do with an inner helpline these days!

You can develop your inner helpline with a mantra, devotion, or a ritual.

A mantra is a sound, a special sound that you cultivate—a sound that carries special meaning to you and therefore a positive emotional shift. This inner change associated with a mantra is called *bhava* in Sanskrit.

That is the most important purpose of a mantra—to recall to the mind that positive inner change.

That positive inner feeling or connection will not grow spontaneously. It has to be nurtured through study and practice and by guidance from a teacher. The attitude you have toward your mantra will determine the effect of using it. The feeling and inner relationship are the key to the mantra.

Reverence and devotion, trust and protection, peace and steadiness, inner strength and well-being—these are all good feelings to cultivate with a mantra. Devoid of this kernel of feeling and meaning, the sound of the mantra is incomplete, like the husk.

As we repeat our mantra, we reinforce the feeling associated with it. The connection between a mantra and its associated feelings becomes deeply internalized.

Thus over time, in or out of meditation, the effect of a mantra can become an internal helpline through which you can unburden your mind at any moment during the day or night.

ALPHABET PRAYER

A small girl was saying "A, B, C, D, E..." reverentially, like a prayer. When the preacher asked what she was doing, she said, "I am praying."

The preacher scolded her and asked her to pray properly. She then replied, "I don't know how to pray. But God knows what I want, and he will arrange the letters and spell out my prayer correctly."

Remove Suffering with Sound

Freedom, known as *moksha* in Sanskrit, is the common goal of most ancient Indian philosophies. Freedom from what? From suffering. To free ourselves from suffering, we need our minds to be unwaveringly steady. An unsteady mind ensures that we will vacillate between pleasure and displeasure.

One pathway to this steadiness of mind is based on sound. The chanting of the mantras, for example, can bring focus to the mind, and we can use that focus to foster reflection on their meaning. This dual practice of focusing the mind combined with reflection will lead to the desired transformation toward inner steadiness.

Why sound? The mind thinks in words; we use language to make sense of the world around us and our relation to it. The mind can be corralled and channeled by replacing that distracted inner chatter with a focused stream of sound, such as mantras.

Let Go; It's Not a Problem

We do not act without expectation. Expectations are a type of projection into the future. We cannot, however, predict the external results of our actions because there are too many factors beyond our control. And when our expectations are unfulfilled—as they often are—we experience unhappiness and suffering.

But we can predict the internal results of our actions, because they depend on our attitude. In yoga, we work with our minds to ensure that the internal results are in our hands.

If we let go of unnecessary and unrealistic expectations internally, in our minds, the anxiety that often accompanies them recedes as well. This brings a sense of peace within.

The fundamental point of yoga is that attaining and keeping a quiet mind is never a waste of time. Mental strength comes from an ongoing practice of unburdening the mind.

If you manage to calm your mind once, you can be confident that you can calm it again. Each daily yoga practice leads you deeper into clarity and peace.

Underpinning this transformation is the attitude of letting go of what we do not need, of what is negative and holding us back.

~~~~~~~~~~

HEAVY THOUGHTS

Several artists were waiting in the elevator of an old studio building in New York. The operator attempted to ascend with the passengers, but the car refused to budge. Several times he opened the gate, asking a few people to wait for the following trip. Still the elevator would not move.

Again the gate was opened, and a very little woman got out. Presto! The elevator began to ascend, but not before the passengers heard the lady explain, "It is not that I weigh so much; it is that I have so much on my mind today."

~~~~~~~~~~~

Know It from Within

Transformation through yoga is not like the Internet; there is no quick download from the guru! There is a famous parable that illustrates this.

A group of ten men on a journey reached a river on their path. They managed to cross the river, and emerging on the other side, they wanted to ensure all ten had made it safely. The last one to cross began counting, and found only nine men. He was alarmed and alerted the others. Each one counted in turn and found only nine!

As they were in tears, mourning their missing companion, a passing sage came upon them and asked them what the problem was.

"Alas, sage!" they cried. "One of us is missing, lost in the treacherous waters of the river!"

The sage smiled and said, "Let me count." And he found ten.

Of course, each person who was counting included everyone but himself. Only with the intervention of the sage, or the guru, were they able to find themselves!

But a key point to note here is that the sage did not bring the tenth man with him. He only pointed out what was already there. The realization was not from outside, but from within. The guru is only the catalyst. The student is the practitioner, the one who has to seek and undergo the transformation.

If we look within ourselves, we will find the one who is missing!

6 *Sampling the Traditional*

Yoga as a Mirror

Yoga is a philosophy, but it is a philosophy informed by direct experience rather than logic or theorizing alone. In Sanskrit, the path of yoga is called a *darshana*, which can be translated as "mirror." A *darshana* is a way of knowing that is based on looking at the roots, nature, connections, and purpose of a subject.

For example, a *darshana* based on the statement "I exist" attempts to answer these questions:

1.   What is the origin of "I exist?"

2.   What is the nature of "I?"

3.   How does "I" relate to me and to others?

Following this scheme, yoga explains the roots, nature, and connections of the mind, body, and world.

The logic of yoga was the result of the direct experiences of sages in the past. What they discovered long ago remains just as effective today because the external world continues to press upon us, and our minds continue to respond in ways that bind us!

Time machine

Space travel to alternate reality

Meditation

Three ways to meet yourself.

Secret of Ancient Yoga Texts

Foremost among ancient yoga texts is Patanjali's Yogasutra, a text consisting of 195 terse aphorisms, or pithy sayings. The Yogasutra, along with traditional commentaries on it, explains the practice of meditation and the psychology of yoga in detail. It offers a systematic method for making the transition from the distracted smind that rules many of our decisions to a steady and peaceful mind that waits upon our command.

Patanjali was able to see the origin of the mind and to understand its nature. He understood that the more freedom we give to the wanderings of the mind, the more we are in bondage to it.

Conversely, the more we steady the mind, the freer we are from its bondage.

From the ancient yoga texts, we learn of the experiences of those who achieved these heightened states of awareness. The fundamentals that these sages have described come from empirical knowledge—from their own experiences, not merely from concepts about the way to achieve peace of mind. Writing out of their enlightened experience, the ancient sages revealed the steps on this path for the benefit of all humanity.

From the verbal testimony of these sages, their followers inferred the wisdom of the path. When these followers undertook the path that the sages described, their direct experience confirmed the wisdom of the sages. They, in turn, perpetuated the wisdom.

In truth, the traditional path of the Yogasutra is not following any tradition. The traditional path is to follow the logic of the text supported by your own practice.

The role of the guru is to help you understand the teachings and guide you in your practice.

Consequently, several traditional Sanskrit commentaries have been written on the Yogasutra. When studying the Yogasutra, keep in mind that the text is not based on faith. You are expected to understand the text by analysis, by practice, and by your own experience.

The *Yoga Yajnavalkya* is an orderly yoga text that dates before many of the other yoga texts such as the *Hatha Yoga Pradipika*. The Yogasutra predates the *Yoga Yajnavalkya*. The Yogasutra is a defining text devoid of any historical or social commentary, but the *Yoga Yajnavalkya* and other yoga texts do contain such messages that are not relevant to the practice of yoga in the twenty-first century. Outside of the Yogasutra and *Yoga Yajnavalkya*, there are no detailed and systematically organized presentations of the eight limbs of yoga. The other yoga texts tend to be disorganized in comparison.

The ancient yoga scriptures are thought by some to contain mystical secrets that are transmitted from teacher to student, but this is not actually true.

The Sanskrit word *rahasya* in these texts does mean "secret." But it is secret not because it can only be mystically transmitted from a guru but because it is not in our comprehension or experience now. With guided study and practice, both understanding and experience will dawn.

Language and Context in Ancient Texts

Language and context are essential for effective communication. Accuracy of language and comprehension of context are all the more important when we are understanding something written hundreds or thousands of years in the past, especially if it is a subject with depth or technicality. All technical subjects have their own lexicon, after all, be they mathematics, philosophy, or classical yoga.

In classical texts, it was expected that the specific technical words used would be defined and their context elaborated on in the commentaries. As a result, the same word may be used in different classical texts with different meanings.

To understand what that word means in a particular text, the reader was supposed to refer the commentaries.

For example, the word yoga is used in the Yogasutra to mean focus. In some other classical texts, it is used to convey the meaning "union." Substituting one meaning for another can result in confusion.

ENJOY YOUR MEAL

An elderly Japanese man was staying at an exclusive vacation resort in Switzerland for the first time. The first night out at dinner, he was at a table with a debonair Frenchman. Before dinner, the Frenchman rose, bowed politely, and said, "Bon appétit."

The Japanese gent bowed in return, replying, "Anami Tanjiro."

The next morning at breakfast, the next noon at lunch, and the next evening at dinner, the ceremony was repeated, and the elderly Japanese was beginning to feel a little confused.

"I don't understand," he told a companion in the lounge. "The Frenchman told me his name, Bon Appétit. I told him my name, Anami Tanjiro. But at every meal he starts all over again."

His friend laughed, "The Frenchman is not introducing himself. 'Bon appétit' is French for 'I hope you have a pleasant meal.'"

The Japanese gentleman breathed a sigh of relief. The next morning when he appeared at the breakfast, he was prepared. Forestalling the Frenchman, he bowed politely and said, "Bon appétit."

Whereupon the Frenchman rose, bowed, and answered, "Anami Tanjiro."

"Ha" "tha" Yoga

Hatha yoga is popular in this day. We have hatha classes, hatha vinyasa, or hatha flow classes in many yoga studios. What is hatha yoga? The most widespread idea is that doing asanas—bending the body into yoga poses—is the practice of hatha yoga. The most well-known text on hatha yoga is the *Hatha Yoga Pradipika* authored in the fifteenth century. Reading the *Hatha Yoga Pradipika*, one cannot fail to appreciate that classical hatha yoga is not merely practicing asanas.

The common meaning of the word hatha is to be stubborn or tenacious—to persist in something with effort. The commentaries on the *Hatha Yoga Pradipika* explain hatha as "with strength." Here, the strength needed is not only mental, in the form of willpower or persistence, but physical strength, too.

The word yoga in hatha yoga texts generally means "union." (Unlike the Yogasutra, where it, more logically and usefully, means "focus.") Union of what? Of the prana represented by the sound "ha" and the apana represented by the sound "tha."

By sustained effort, both physical and mental, while the person is young and strong, the yogi unites the forces or energies of the prana and apana.

However, in truth, these are not two separate functions or energies; they are two aspects of the same one. By channeling the flow of prana, the flow of the mind is also channeled, and vice versa; the mind becomes focused.

Further, the sound "ha" also refers to the sun and the sound "tha" to the moon, or heating and cooling at the body level. The foundation for both of them is *agni*, the metabolism at the level of the body. What brings them together is *vayu* or air; in the body, that is the movement of the life force or prana.

The prana moves through the channel to the right of the spine center, called the *pingala*. The apana moves through the channel to the left of the spine center, called the *ida*. To bring these the prana and apana together, that is, to channel the flow of apana in the central nadi called the *sushumna*, is hatha yoga.

Make Prana Go into Sushumna

The Sanskrit name of some well-known asanas contains the word *tana*. For example, *uttanasana* (standing forward bend) or *pascimatanasana* (seated forward bend). The word *tana* means "to extend." This word is commonly translated as a stretch because "to stretch" and "to extend" seem close in meaning. From here we get the meaning that *pascimatanasana* is to stretch the back body: *pascima*: back, *tana*: stretch. This goes with the form of the asana as a seated forward bend, which stretches the back body.

However, there is a deeper layer of understanding beyond the musculoskeletal level.

The word tana here refers not just to the stretch of the muscles but to the extension of the flow of prana or subtle awareness of life force.

Where is the prana flow extended? In to the central pathway in the back or the spine, the *sushumna*.

The commentary on *pascimatanasana* in the *Hatha Yoga Pradipika* says that the purpose of this asana is to make the prana flow in the back or in reverse. That is, the prana, which is normally scattered through the body, is brought back into the *sushumna* and made to flow there. The awareness of the gross body diminishes, and awareness of the subtle body within increases.

This cannot be done only by bending the body; it also requires controlling the breath and focusing the mind. That is why some of these postures are meant to be done with long breathing, suspension of the breath, and extended stay. Doing asanas in this way requires a deeper level of preparation and experience than can be achieved purely by looking at the bones, muscles, and fascia.

What Is Prana?

The mind is an experience—the experience of thoughts and emotions. Looking at your mind, you can see thoughts and feelings passing through it in rapid succession. But for the functioning of the mind, body, and senses, we need energy or life force.

This subtle life force that we cannot see with our eyes or other gross senses is given the name prana.

This prana is responsible for all life functions, and in turn, is rooted in the presence of consciousness behind the body and mind. Our connection with our mind and body begins with that feeling, "I," but that is not the prana. That feeling "I" lies at the root of our experiences in the mind and body. We notice happy thoughts and feelings in the mind. We notice unhappy thoughts and feelings in the mind. We feel pleasantness, tiredness, or pain in the body.

We taste the food we eat and enjoy it. But once the food is in our stomach and intestines, we do not perceive all the steps of it being digested.

The functions of the prana are usually not within our direct experience, yet we understand through inference that these life functions are proceeding within us.

If I don't want to see something, I can close my eyes and prevent my eyes from seeing it. However, once I have ingested a meal, I cannot decide not to digest it. "Let me stop the digestion of the food within me that is happening now" is not an actionable goal for an ordinary person. That is, the functioning of prana is generally outside of our direct voluntary control.

The root of the word prana means "to lead or to go." The flux that forms the basis of life, the constant momentary changes that happen in the body, mind, and senses, is led and supported by the prana.

We cannot stop this flux or flow of life force, or prana; we can only direct or channel it.

Instead of prana being scattered, we can direct it to bring about specific transformation in the body and mind. As the prana is the support for the constant changes in the mind, channeling the prana can provide the basis for focusing and channeling the mind as well.

Classical hatha yoga describes the method of doing this.

To channel the prana and control the mind, we have to transform the activity of the body, breath, and senses. Asana transforms the body along with the breath. Pranayama works on the breath exclusively with the bandhas. The senses are contained by the practice of listening to the inner sound (*nadanusandhana*) with the shanmukhi mudra. The mind is brought to absorption on this inner sound in time.

Consciousness, Prana, and the Mind

The body and mind function because of the presence of consciousness or life. In its absence, the body and mind cease to function. That power that causes the mind, body, and senses to function is the prana or life force. In truth, we infer the presence of prana or life force because our minds, bodies, and senses are functioning.

Similarly, in the presence of consciousness, we experience thoughts and feelings. Desires and dislikes arise in our awareness, and we act on the basis of these thoughts and feelings. This power of cognition and will is the mind.

But if cognition and will are to function, they require the prana or life force to be present.

The prana and the mind are intertwined. The rise and fall of thoughts in the mind requires the function of prana, the energy behind it.

To see something with our eyes, and for that image to be transmitted to the mind, the life force or prana is required. But to recognize that image and decide what to do with it is the function of the mind.

Hatha yoga described how we can channel the prana that lies behind the functioning of the mind and thereby channel the mind.

We would all like to be free of suffering or unhappiness. The path to that goal requires control over mind and prana. In this, the role of the mind is dominant. For even to do the asanas and pranayama that will help us control the prana, the direction of the mind is essential. Furthermore, the mind is within our direct experience, while the prana is largely not. We are able to say, "I am thinking of this." But we are not able to appreciate the function of the prana like that. We are not able to directly experience our prana behind the secretion of hormones in our body.

In the same way, we are able to change what we think or feel in our minds directly. We can choose to think certain thoughts or experience certain emotions. We may not be able to sustain them because our minds are unsteady, but in a given moment, it is amenable to our direct control. But we cannot normally direct the functions of the prana concretely like that; we cannot decide to move the flow of blood more to one kidney than the other!

Hatha yoga gives importance to the control of prana, and through that the mind. But we must note that it is not possible to control the prana effectively without the attention and oversight by the mind. Thus the *Hatha Yoga Pradipika* cautions against working with the prana without the accompanying required focus of the mind. Asanas, pranayama, and the mudras will bear fruit only if practiced with a focused mind. Only then are they truly a limb of yoga.

> *Hatha yoga says, first control the prana, and by that, the mind will become focused.*

By the hatha yoga practices of asana, pranayama, and mudras, the mind will become steady and fit for the practice of meditation (*dharana*) as described in the Yogasutra. Then you will be able to access the deeper meditative state of *samadhi*, and eventually transcend the flux of the mind. Thus the practice of hatha yoga becomes a pathway to the raja yoga described by Patanjali in the Yogasutra.

What Does Uniting Prana and Apana Mean?

Generally, when two objects or forces unite, they lose their distinct qualities and identities and take on a composite nature instead.

Prana and apana are not two separate forces or entities. They are two aspects of the same force, represented in the breath as inhalation and exhalation.

There is only one breath, of which inhale and exhale are two aspects. We can think of it like temperature. For example, temperature is merely a fact of the environment. But when it is greater than our body temperature, we say it is hot, and when it is less than our body temperature, we say it is cool.

Similarly, the classical texts separate the unitary breath into two components, the prana, connected to the sun, and the apana, connected to the moon. This division is representative, not absolute.

When the unitary prana flows in both right and left channels as prana and apana, the mind is scattered. When the unitary prana, meaning both prana and apana, flow in the center channel known as *sushumna*, the mind is centered and focused.

The above explanation does have several technical words, often in Sanskrit. To understand this subject in depth, the classical texts and studies provide for each word the precise definition, expansion on their import, the connections between them, the relation between these and the mind, and their role on the path to transcendence or *moksha*.

Now, what is the connection between the control and steadiness of the mind described in the Yogasutra and the hatha yoga ideas and practice described above?

To understand hatha yoga, we must know this first: What is prana? What is the connection between prana and the mind? There is much confusion surrounding the topic of prana, but this topic isn't really that difficult.

The pathway of classical hatha yoga comprises the following steps or branches:

1. The practitioner must learn and practice asanas under the eye of a wise teacher. While doing asanas, he must also learn how to combine and use breathing effectively along with the body movement and positions. And from here, he must also master the practice of the bandhas.

2. While learning the asanas, the practitioner must also develop the practice of pranayama.

3. When doing pranayama, the practitioner must include the bandhas and by that practice bring the mind to a point of steady focus.

4. By the above practices, the *nadis* or channels through which prana or life force flows in the body become clear. When the *nadis* are purified and the practitioner is able to remain in the pranayama with the bandhas, awareness of the subtle flow of the prana in the body arises. The mind is absorbed in the subtle sound or sensation of this flow of prana and becomes ready to stay steady in deep meditation or *samadhi*. This process is known as *nadanusandhana* or listening to the inner

sound. It may also be called *laya yoga* or the yoga of inner absorption.

5. Thus, the practice of hatha yoga becomes a pathway to raja yoga, the yoga described by Patanjali in the Yogasutra. In other words, this hatha yoga leads to deep focus of the mind, and the different states of meditation or *samadhi* described in the Yogasutra.

To Be Successful in Hatha Yoga

To be successful in the practices of hatha yoga, the following are required:

1. Youth. The practitioner must be young, not middle aged.

2. The right teacher who can guide the student through the steps of practice.

3. Devoting all of one's time to the practice with no other activities in the day.

4. Strict control over diet and other sense impulses.

5. Sustained practice for several years with a right teacher.

Aspirants who meet all the above criteria are very rare, and finding a teacher who can teach this is equally rare. Consequently, it is difficult to find a person who is truly successful in this practice.

A point to remember is that while the word hatha refers to stubbornness or persistence in the practice as well as the physical

Pandas are probably more fun.

strength required to do the practices like the bandhas comfortably, it does not mean blind coercion or compulsion.

It does not mean forceful practice, but a practice where a degree of strength is necessary for success.

IT'S EASY

A man passing through a small town saw indications of amazing marksmanship all about on trees, barns, and fences, each with a bullet hole in the exact center of a target. He asked to meet the expert shot.

"This is sensational. How in the world did you do it?" asked the visitor.

"Easy as pie" was the answer. "I shoot first and draw the circles afterward."

7 *Examining the Esoteric*

Sleep and Samadhi

The phrase *yoga nidra* occurs in ancient texts. Literally, it means "yogic sleep." This is a paradoxical phrase. The state of yoga is one of present moment awareness. But when sleeping, we have no awareness of the moment! What, then, is yogic sleep?

What the ancient texts mean by this phrase is the state of *samadhi* or absolute inner focus. Superficially, a yogi in *samadhi* appears to be unaware of his surroundings, just like a person who is asleep. But there is an important difference between sleep and *samadhi*. In sleep, there is no clear awareness of anything, outside or inside. In *samadhi*, while the yogi may be unaware of the outside, he is intensely aware of the object of his focus inside.

The modern practice called *yoga nidra* is principally a relaxation technique, usually based on moving relaxed attention through the body. It is usually done lying down or in a supported posi-

Come closer folks! He is in samadhi. He meditates every day after lunch.

TIGER SAFARI

tion. The goal of the practice is relaxation rather than meditation.

Focused meditation, in contrast, is best done in a seated posture. Standing, the body is too unstable and prone to movement. Lying down, the mind slips into a state of decreased awareness too easily.

A seated posture with the spine upright is the ideal base for meditation. Relaxation, in contrast, is best done lying down, for we are happy to accept a state of decreased awareness in relaxation.

Indeed, that's the goal of relaxation—to reduce the hypervigilance that accompanies anxiety.

If relaxation ends in sleep, we are not dismayed. Meditation ending in sleep, however, is not a success! Sleep is a barrier to effective meditation. Relaxation has wonderful benefits, but it is quite different from meditation, and not a substitute for it.

He Is Me

We identify with many things in our lives. The path of yoga is a way to wake up and find ourselves! This parable illustrates, in a lighter vein, the paradox that we face in our lives:

A man stayed in a dormitory for a night. He told his neighbor, "I'm afraid I might get lost when I am asleep. How can I find myself when I awake?"

His neighbor suggested, "Tie a balloon to your leg tonight. In the morning, when you get up, you can be identified with the help of the balloon."

The man went to sleep with the balloon tied to his leg. His neighbor, wanting to play a joke on him, removed the balloon from the man's leg during the night and tied it to his own leg.

The next morning, the man woke to see the balloon tied to his neighbor's leg, and he cried aloud. When the others asked why, he said, "Seeing the balloon, I know that he is me, but I don't know who I am. If he is me, who am I?"

Anjali Mudra

Look at the picture of Krishnamacharya in anjali mudra. The gaze is downward, classically known as gaze toward the tip of the nose. Anjali mudra may be done for oneself, or as an offering, meditating on the Divine in the heart.

There is an ancient way of expressing the goal of yoga practice. It is part metaphor, part instruction. When we hear the word heart in ancient yoga texts and the Upanishads, it does not refer to the physical organ pumping away beneath our chests. Instead, it refers to the space within the center of the chest, the space where emotions seem to resonate and the center of our identities seem to reside in our bodies. That's where we point when we say "I." We place our hands on our hearts and point our fingers toward that center of the chest when talk about our feelings, be they sadness or happiness.

In that heart center, the mind is conceptualized as a lotus flower, closed and upside down. In anjali mudra, we bring the fingers of our two hands together, the base of the palms touching, with the knuckles apart from each other.

The palms are not flat against each other but are shaped like the bud of a flower.

This represents that lotus flower, pointing upward, as if our hearts were raised and righted. Ready to open like a beautiful lotus flowering in the light of the sun, our hearts and minds are purified, ready to open in the light of the teachings and practice.

In many asanas where the hands are free, we can do the anjali mudra. It represents that journey within, an intention of trust and surrender.

Try doing asanas with and without this anjali mudra, with and without that feeling inside the heart. You will notice the difference.

Attitude is a little thing, but it makes a big difference.

Traditionally, we do this anjali mudra as a gesture of respect to those that enlightened and enriched our hearts and minds, to our parents, to our gurus, and to the Divine. We place the hands in different regions of the body to symbolize our connection with those individuals. To our mothers, the anjali mudra could be in front of the navel, for mothers give life. To the guru, the anjali mudra could be in front of the lips, for it is the words of the guru that enlighten. To the Divine, the anjali mudra could be over the head, for it is by the grace of the Divine that body and mind can function in this world.

Thus, as an act of complete trust and surrender to the will of the Divine, we can use prostration with the anjali mudra by laying ourselves on the ground, facing downward, with our arms stretched overhead with the anjali mudra. With this act, we offer ourselves, from head to toe, to the care of the Divine.

The point underlying the anjali mudra in all contexts is developing the sense of humility and reducing the ego.

By adding this simple mudra in our practice, we can remind ourselves to stay grounded and ensure our yoga practices or our lives do not become a source of unhealthy pride but instead an act of offering and grace.

WHAT'S IN A NAME?

A celebrity strolling on a beach near her summer home stopped to chat with a little girl playing in the sand. The child slipped her small hand in the celebrity's, and they walked together on the beach.

After some time the little girl said, "I have to go home now."

"Good-bye, dear," said the celebrity. "When your mother asks you where you were, tell her you were walking with Marion West."

"And when your folks ask where you were," said the child, "tell them that you were walking with Gail Parker."

Yoga Mudra

This mudra is also called *cin mudra* or *jnana mudra*. There is a well-known story behind this mudra. Siva, representing the Divine, once took the form of a boy of sixteen. Seated, absorbed in meditation, with an aura of deep calm, and radiant in appearance, he was approached by sages who saw through his disguise and recognized his true nature. The sages asked with reverence, "What is the essence of the Vedas and all spiritual teaching?" Siva gave no answer, but he showed them this simple mudra: he raised his palm toward them and brought his index finger down to join its tip to his thumb.

The sages understood what he was saying, though he had never said a word! The guru's discourse was silence, but the students' doubts were dispelled.

So what did the sages understand from this simple mudra? The index finger is the individual—the self or the ego. The thumb is the Divine. The other three fingers are the three qualities of the mind and nature (*satva*, *rajas*, and *tamas*). When the mind moves away from the flux of these qualities and reaches stillness, the individual is united with the Divine nature within.

This mudra is called cin mudra because the word *cit* (which becomes *cin* when joined with the word *mudra*) means "consciousness."

This mudra says let go of the ego of the mind, and you will experience the true nature of consciousness.

This mudra is also known as the *jnana mudra*, the word *jnana* meaning "to know"—to know one's true nature or the nature of the Divine, that is.

Classically, the explanation of this mudra involves the Divine and the idea of joining with it. While the anjali mudra is useful to define the attitude of humbleness in the practice, this yoga mudra points to the goal that is at the end of the practice.

However, Krishnamacharya was generally not in the habit of recommending this mudra when doing pranayama. You will notice that holding any hand position in pranayama can potentially be a distraction. As your focus on the breath deepens, the more natural the position of the limbs, the easier the absorption of the mind. You need to keep only the spine comfortably upright and the body stable; this is necessary to ensure that the breath flows smoothly. Of course, if this mudra helps you stay more mindful, you can certainly incorporate it in your practice.

Inward focus of the gaze—the direction of the eyes—is important, though, in both pranayama and meditation.

Look at the ancient depictions of the Buddha or other meditations. You will see the meditators gazing a little inward with the palms usually placed comfortably one atop the other. The spine, though, will always be upright.

Shanmukhi Mudra

There are six gateways to experience the world: the five senses and the mind. Thus there are six gateways to distraction as well. The alternating restless and dullness of the senses, and their controller from within, the mind, are the source of the constant flux in our life experience.

Cut down the incessant buzz of the senses. Repeatedly draw the mind to a steady object within.

And we have laid the platform to build the steadiness of mind required for sustained meditation.

An external mudra that signifies this intention is the shanmukhi mudra. The idea behind this mudra is to shut off the external sense organs with the fingers. To do this mudra, you bring your hands up to your face. Place your thumbs over the opening of the ears, the index and middle fingers over the closed eyelids, and narrow the nostrils with the ring fingers.

This practice begins as a form of *pratyahara*, the fifth limb in the eight limbs of yoga, and may deepen further into meditation.

Pratyahara consists of drawing the senses away from their objects so that the mind can be focused without distraction.

One way to do this is to give the senses a steady object of focus that is within one's own body, so that attention does not scatter outward. This practice of listening to an inner sound (*nadanusandhana*) is one such.

But this practice is not about producing a sound within and listening to it. That is, we don't close our ears and hum, for example! While that can temporarily provide us something to listen to, that isn't the inner sound the *Hatha Yoga Pradipika* is speaking of. In fact, the sound of humming is an outer sound, like speaking.

The inner sound the *Hatha Yoga Pradipika* refers to is a more subtle awareness of the sound that arises after extended pranayama, when the *nadis* or channels of life force are clear, and the mind is capable of appreciating the subtle sensations of the body.

In that state of mind, we can perceive the subtle sounds of the body, and even deeper, the origin of sound itself. If we concentrate the mind on the nature of that sound, we begin to realize the nature of sense perception itself, for we perceive the difference between the awareness in the mind and the sensation of sound. That takes us into deeper meditation.

In this process, the position of the hands or even the mudra itself, is not the key. After all, we cannot force our awareness within by just physically closing the eyes and ears. The mind will still wander, and there is no guarantee of the subtle awareness of the body awakening within us.

Thus, the mudra itself is only a marker of the intention and an external support. The key is inner awareness and the prior practice of pranayama.

Validate Claims

The classical hatha yoga texts (*Hatha Yoga Pradipika, Gheranda Samhita, Yoga Upanishads*, etc.) contain useful information. But they also contain claims and hyperbole intended to make yoga more compelling to a student. These claims are

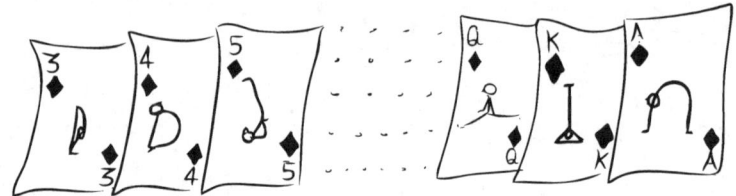

A yoga pack. Four aces! Four kings and queens! Is there a joker too?

meant to be interpreted by a qualified teacher, not followed literally.

As always, you need to apply logic and your own good sense, apart from relying on the wisdom of a sound teacher, to see if these claims make sense.

For example, the *Hatha Yoga Pradipika* says that anyone can practice yoga, old or sick. But it does not say what practice exactly these people should do, nor does it say that they should all do the same practice. Again, common sense would suggest that while some principles of teaching an arthritic eighty-year-old and a youthfully energetic twenty-year-old may be the same, it would be unwise to make them do the exact same movements and breathing.

BE WISE

Wife: "Minerva was the goddess of wisdom."

Husband: "To whom was she married?"

Wife: "She was the goddess of wisdom. She did not get married."

Sun, Moon, and Other Salutations

There can be hardly a yoga student who is not familiar with asana sequences called sun salutation. The idea of sun salutation is an ancient one across many cultures. It finds a place in Vedic literature too. The Vedic notion of a prayer to the sun is symbolic—the sun represents the Divine, or one's own consciousness. It is not actually worship of the sun per se. This ritual or prayer has its own mantras and structure. The Vedic sun salutation ritual, however, does not include the asana sequences we see under that name nowadays.

Similarly, many ancient rituals follow the cycle of the moon. One phase of the ritual is done on the rising moon and the other on the waning moon. In Vedic thought, if the sun represents consciousness, the moon represents the mind.

Consciousness is ever present like the sun. The mind is ever changing, like the moon.

Like the moon is illuminated by the light of the sun, the mind functions in the presence of consciousness. Again, there is no moon-salutation asana sequence in ancient Vedic literature.

However, these phases of the moon or the rising and setting of the sun do not have much to do with the practice of classical yoga. From the yoga perspective, all days are good days to practice! As Krishnamacharya used to say, "If you eat food, you practice!" Meaning that just as we eat food to nourish the body every day, we must also do yoga to balance the mind every day.

Krishnamacharya On Posture-Remedy Relationship

In an interview in 1984:

> Q. In modern therapy, a doctor prescribes a specific drug for a specific disease. In yoga therapy, can we prescribe one asana for each particular disease?

> A. No. We cannot say that this asana or this pranayama can be given for this disease. This is because the treatment is given based on pranayama and restraint of *ahara* (food); the treatment may not be effective if these primary constraints are not complied with. Complete rooting out of the disease will not be possible unless pranayama, asana, and *ahara* are combined properly and practiced. Certainly, we cannot state that the formula of one disease-one asana or pranayama is valid in *yoga cikitsa* (yoga therapy). In hatha yoga, and in the *Yoga Upanishads*, examples are given for males and females of specific asanas to be practiced for every disease. But this is not practicable, since many variety of diseases are there. In the *Puranas*, examples are cited wherein brothers fight among themselves and afterward, following the path of yoga they get over their illnesses. There are many diseases, and particular asanas are identified to cure them in the *Puranas*. Again, in the *Hatha Yoga Pradipika*, we find *paschimottanasana* can cure certain diseases.

We must evaluate under what bodily conditions, at what age, in what countries, and in whom this asana can cure a disease in the body.

But after all the descriptions of asanas, they always talk about *vairagya*. If any practitioner of yoga wants to remove any disability or disease, he must practice *vairagya* (non-attachment). Otherwise, the treatment will not be effective. He again gets the disease. Thus, asanas are not effective either, though there are innumerable pranayamas. Thus, one asana for one disease is an impracticable formula.

Soil, Sunlight, and the Seed

I have been asked more than once, if students learned yoga from the same teacher, why are their own teachings not the same?

Fundamentally, the material or direct cause for transformation is the intention and capacity of the student. A student cannot be transformed unless the seed of that transformation already exists within her.

Even the most skilled or well-regarded teacher of yoga can never be the direct cause of a student's transformation. A teacher can only be an indirect cause of a student's progress, or may not be a cause at all. The teacher can provide the student with the tools for transformation, but the student must be the doer.

This does not diminish the importance of the yoga teacher as a guide. But, ultimately, progress in controlling the mind must be accomplished by the student's own effort.

A teacher can offer only knowledge, clarity, inspiration, and support by example and presence.

The seed within a lemon has the potential to become a lemon tree. Suppose the seed does sprout and become a tree. The direct, or material, cause was the seed's inherent potential to become a tree. An indirect, or supportive, cause was the sunlight that nourished the sprout.

A lemon seed and apple seed will both be nurtured by soil, water, and sunlight but yield different fruit. Similarly, practices will create different transformations in individual students depending on their motivations and characters. What the student brings to the practice is as important as the practice itself.

In other words, the direct cause of a student's transformation is that student's inherent capacity to understand, absorb, and carry out the principles of a yoga practice.

A teacher can only guide the student on the path. He or she cannot directly cause a student's transformation.

Another way to think of the teacher is as a kind of scaffold rather than the bricks and mortar. The bricks and mortar represent the essential qualities of a student that enable him to learn.

When the scaffold is removed, the bricks and mortar are expected to stand on their own. So it is with yoga.

For example, I am one of Krishnamacharya's few long-term students. Krishnamacharya gave me a mantra and many other practices. But it is I who had to work with that mantra and those practices over years to seek the transformation they can create.

As practitioners, we have to look within ourselves and see what changes are happening inside— how the knowledge we receive impacts us—and discern our own motivations and boundaries.

The teacher cannot decide these for us, nor will these be the same across students.

Transformation in a student is a matter of cause and effect. This was recognized and emphasized by the ancient yoga sages.

In yoga, then and now, there is no effect without a logical cause. There are no accidents, only incidents.

In Indian logic, there are two categories of causes for things that happen in life:

- direct, or material, causes and
- indirect, or supportive, causes.

Why is it important to understand this distinction? One reason is to discourage students from idealizing a yoga teacher, making the teacher into an icon, or placing unreasonable expectations on a teacher. A student whose focus and attachment is on the teacher rather than on the practice will miss the benefits of the practice.

A second reason is to resist the human tendency to believe what someone says solely because that person is in a position of authority. Belief must be grounded in experience. A student must be willing to test and authenticate what a teacher says.

The third reason is that we all have a tendency to resist the hard work of growth and change. The process of transformation requires patience, humility, and discipline. It is easy to understand the wish to avoid the effort by having a teacher transform us with a gesture or a word or a magic wand. But we must be the doer. There is no other option.

WORTHINESS OF THE STUDENT

A little boy stood watching the balloon man at the country fair. There were all shapes of balloons in all colors. The seller let loose a brown balloon. It soared high into the air.

Many people were attracted by the incident. The vendor thought that it might be good business to let another go. So he let a bright yellow one slip free. It soared higher. Then he released a green one. It soared high until it could scarcely be seen.

The little boy stood looking for a long time at the rising balloons. Then he asked, "Sir, if you sent the blue one up, would it go as high as the others?"

The balloon man said with a smile, "Sonny, it isn't the color or shape; it's the stuff inside that makes it rise."

What Is a Secret?

When two politicians, corporate heads, or lovers are behind closed doors, we know that what is happening, in one sense. We may not have the details, but we do have a general idea. It is not entirely a secret in that sense.

In the Bhagavad Gita, we find Krishna telling Arjuna, "This is the secret of all secrets," but what is secret about it when the text is available to everyone to hear and read?

Similarly, ancient mantras are often supposed to be secret and are received behind closed doors from a guru. Again, what is secret about them if they are available for everyone to hear? And now, we can listen to them as a digital download!

The point here is that the inner meaning is not revealed by simply saying it; the inner meaning is the actual secret.

But books are available now, explaining the meaning of mantras. How can it still remain a secret?

It can because the revelation of a mantra's true meaning is not in words but in an experience. That experience can be earned only through personal effort.

The meaning is hidden in the cave of your heart, and your personal practice is the key that unlocks it.

Doubt (Is) the Teacher

All of us want knowledge that is accurate. None of us want knowledge that is incorrect. We cannot have both correct and incorrect knowledge about one particular issue at one time if those pieces of knowledge are opposed. Or can we?

Doubt is an important component that helps us move from inaccurate to accurate understanding.

If we never have any doubts, we may remain stuck in an inaccurate understanding indefinitely.

That can be a real problem if that inaccurate understanding is related to our own personal growth and transformation.

Of course, we can take doubt to an extreme where it is crippling. But doubt is a valuable component of personal growth so long as it's not crippling.

When we encourage a sense of healthy inquiry, we open the possibility of growth.

NO DOUBTS POSSIBLE

Three year old John was busy scribbling something on a piece of paper.

His mother called out to him, "John, what are you doing?"

John replied, "I'm writing a letter to Michael, mama." Michael was his younger brother, just a year old.

Amused, his mother said, "But you don't know how to write!"

John replied, "Oh, that's alright. He doesn't know how to read!"

Are You Ready?

A student wrote to me, "My teacher said that I was not ready to receive the teachings on self-realization."

In the ancient texts, this is a common refrain. The student asks the teacher, "Teach me the means to self-realization." The teacher replies, "Practice and come back in a year (or ten years)."

Practice what? Usually the instruction is to practice control over the senses and meditation or contemplation.

When the student returns, the teacher gives him a piece of wisdom and suggests that he contemplate and practice further. This continues step by step until the student finally reaches his goal of self-realization.

Self-transformation does not come in compact modules. It comes through an incremental process by way of your practice with the guidance of the teacher.

Appendix: A Journey Through Yoga

My teacher was the yogi Tirumalai Krishnamacharya (1888-1989), a spiritual practitioner of rare mastery. He had a great thirst for knowledge and a matching capacity for learning. Even as a boy, Krishnamacharya had a sharp mind and a deep curiosity, and was an exceptional student. Trained in the study of the Vedas, an ancient body of knowledge, Krishnamacharya also learned the fundamentals of yoga from his father.

He studied Sanskrit grammar and logic at Queens College in Benares, while continuing the practice of yoga as taught by his father. He then went on to obtain a university degree in yoga theory and *Samkhya* philosophy (the oldest among Eastern philosophies). Krishnamacharya next went to Tibet to study yoga with the yogi Ramamohana Brahmachari. For the majority of the next seven years, Krishnamacharya studied the Yogasutra and further *Samkhya* philosophy and practiced asanas and pranayama under his tutelage.

After his study in Tibet, Krishnamacharya returned to India and obtained several additional university degrees in Eastern philosophies. He then began giving lectures and demonstrations on yoga, and began accepting students. Under the patronage of the maharaja of Mysore, Krishnamacharya directed the *yoga shala* in the Jaganmohan Palace. He eventually moved to Chennai, where my wife and I lived.

Sri T. Krishnamacharya is now recognized by many as the foremost authority in the field of hatha yoga knowledge and practice and is often called "the father of modern yoga."

I was trained as an engineer but was interested in spiritual pursuits. In 1971, I attended a lecture given by Krishnamacharya and was struck by his extraordinary vitality, authoritative presence, and his encyclopedic knowledge of yoga. He was more than eighty years old at that time, but had the constitution of a man twenty years younger.

In 1971, I began my study with him, which continued until his demise in 1989.

In 1971, I began learning asanas and pranayama. This was followed by studies on the Upanishads from 1973 to 1974, covering the *Prasnopanishad, Mundakopanishad,* and others.

In 1975, having attained proficiency in the practice of asanas, Krishnamacharya began teaching me the theory behind asana practice, and composed a series of verses on yoga known as the *Yoganjalisaaram.* We then began classes on yoga therapy.

My study of the Yogasutra also formally commenced in 1975, and continued until Krishnamacharya's demise in 1989.

From 1975 to 1976, Krishnamacharya explained a very interesting text, the *Yoga Yajnavalkya* (which I would go on to translate into English twenty-five years later).

Continuing with studies on hatha yoga over the next two years from 1976 to 1977, I had verse by verse classes on the most well-known text on this topic, the *Hatha Yoga Pradipika*.

For three years, from 1976 to 1979, we undertook a detailed study of an essential text, the Bhagavad Gita.

As my studies on the Bhagavad Gita were going on, Krishnamacharya felt that it was time to go to the roots of the subject, and so, from 1977 to 1978, he explained the *Samkhya Karika*, taking up each verse, as it is such a dense text.

Through a span of almost fifteen years, from 1975 to 1989, we continued to do Vedic chanting regularly.

In 1979, using an upcoming seminar in Europe as an excuse, I persuaded Krishnamacharya to go into the topic of pranayama in detail, including the more esoteric and complex techniques that he had earlier been reluctant to teach.

In 1980, Krishnamacharya delivered a series of in-depth classes over several months, on yoga and Ayurveda, focusing on their therapeutic applications.

From 1980 to 1981, our attention turned to Vedic rituals, their symbolism and uses, looking into sources such as the *Gayatri Ramayana*, and examining the daily Vedic practices such as *Sandhyavandana*.

From 1981 to 1982, we returned to the topic of hatha yoga, taking up the *Gheranda Samhita* and the esoteric practices in the third and fourth chapters of the *Hatha Yoga Pradipika*. This time, as I had already studied most of the hatha yoga techniques, Krishnamacharya chose to do a comparative exposition of the hatha yoga texts, adding his own explanations and notes. This period of study has been greatly illuminating to me years later, when I have looked through his explanations again. At that time, I did not understand the nuances of all his explanations, sometimes derived from his practice and experience in the 1910s and 1920s. But in the later years, as I reviewed what he had said, I began to understand the connections much more clearly.

In 1982, we returned to the study of philosophy with the *Yoga Taravali* of Sri Sankara.

The following year, in 1983, Krishnamacharya turned his attention to the very interesting topic of Vedic phonetics, going through key points from the works of Panini, and adding excerpts from the *Taittiriya Pratishakya*.

In 1985, there was one more round of classes and cases on yoga and Ayurveda as therapy.

Krishnamacharya continued to teach all through his last years. From 1986 to 1989, my studies gradually veered toward the deeper aspects of spiritual practice, looking at *yantras*, mantras, some Tantra rituals, the *Taittiriya Upanishad,* and *Narayana Upanishad.*

In general, over the years of my study with Krishnamacharya, classes on three or more topics would be on-going. Studies of most texts spanned around six months to three years, two to three hours a week, depending on the text.

Krishnamacharya's demise in 1989 was naturally a major shift in my life. I had been studying with him almost every day for so many years. But now my teacher was no more.

I had attempted to extract key principles from Krishnamacharya's teaching in my book, *Yoga for Body, Breath, and Mind*, receiving a foreword from him. That book was published in 1993.

For around six years, from 1990 to 1995, I continued to consolidate what I had learned from the master, and to preserve this knowledge, prepared manuals on yoga, spanning eight volumes on philosophy, wellness, and therapy.

Krishnamacharya was familiar with Ayurveda and its applications, but he was not a practicing Ayurvedic physician. I felt the need to spend some more years studying this subject in depth. So, I returned to study classical Ayurveda in detail, over the six years from 1995 to 2000.

While Krishnamacharya valued the text *Yoga Yajnavalkya* highly, and it was certainly the most organized text on the eight limbs of yoga outside the Yogasutra, it seemed to draw little attention from other yoga schools. I felt it was important to make the text known to a wider audience. Hence, in 1999, with the assistance of my family, I translated the *Yoga Yajnavalkya* into English.

From 2001 to 2004, my studies veered toward a broad swathe of applications of ancient techniques to health and wellness, particularly psychological problems. The Ayurvedic approach to mental disorders was a starting point. From there I went to look at Indian dramatics, particularly emotions and their relation to mental wellness. Then on to Vedic astrology and its use in therapy, and revisiting classical Vedic mantras as therapeutic modalities.

Over this period, I also authored the book *Yoga Therapy* with my wife Indra, son Ganesh, and daughter Nitya.

After the book came out, from 2005 to 2007, the application of *Nyaya* (ancient Indian logic) to philosophy and Ayurveda was the focus of my studies.

Following this, I spent time examining Tantra and Kundalini, practices, starting from the uniting practice of controlling the prana, and looking at it from the various angles of Vedic, Ayurvedic, and yogic perspectives.

Gradually, in 2008, I began to reintegrate what I had studied all these years, going back to roots of *Samkhya*, the Upanishads, and the commentaries on the Yogasutra. I followed this with a comparative study of non-dualism, Buddhism, yoga, *Samkhya*, *Nyaya*, etc.

In 2009, I authored *Krishnamacharya: His Life and Teachings* with Ganesh, which came out the following year. In 2013, we revised the translation of the *Yoga Yajnavalkya* and released a second edition of the work.

These last few years, I have been reflecting and working on drawing together these strands of knowledge. The role of the mind, of wisdom and choice, in determining our life path, has always been a topic of great interest to me, more so now than ever. The needs of modern life are such that mind management is of paramount importance. It is here that the wisdom from the past is particularly helpful.

I still continue to learn, reflect, and practice every day. Krishnamacharya used to say that learning must never stop. A teacher, he felt, must always acquire knowledge and wisdom.

The pathway of yoga is one of constant enquiry and enrichment. Wisdom and clarity arise from the integration of study with guidance, practice with reflection, and experience with minding one's mind.

Let us carry the message of the ancients forward, meaningfully, with discernment and growth.

Made in the USA
San Bernardino, CA
18 April 2015